TAYLOR
E A S Y G U I T A R

ISBN 978-1-7051-2464-2

For all works contained herein:
Unauthorized copying, arranging, adapting, recording, internet posting, public performance,
or other distribution of the music in this publication is an infringement of copyright.
Infringers are liable under the law.

Visit Hal Leonard Online at
www.halleonard.com

Contact us:
Hal Leonard
7777 West Bluemound Road
Milwaukee, WI 53213
Email: info@halleonard.com

In Europe, contact:
Hal Leonard Europe Limited
42 Wigmore Street
Marylebone, London, W1U 2RN
Email: info@halleonardeurope.com

In Australia, contact:
Hal Leonard Australia Pty. Ltd.
4 Lentara Court
Cheltenham, Victoria, 3192 Australia
Email: info@halleonard.com.au

STRUM AND PICK PATTERNS

This chart contains the suggested strum and pick patterns that are referred to by number at the beginning of each song in this book. The symbols ⊓ and ∨ in the strum patterns refer to down and up strokes, respectively. The letters in the pick patterns indicate which right-hand fingers play which strings.

p = **thumb**
i = **index finger**
m = **middle finger**
a = **ring finger**

For example; Pick Pattern 2
is played: thumb - index - middle - ring

Strum Patterns

Pick Patterns

You can use the 3/4 Strum and Pick Patterns in songs written in compound meter (6/8, 9/8, 12/8, etc.). For example, you can accompany a song in 6/8 by playing the 3/4 pattern twice in each measure. The 4/4 Strum and Pick Patterns can be used for songs written in cut time (¢) by doubling the note time values in the patterns. Each pattern would therefore last two measures in cut time.

4	Back to December
10	Blank Space
14	Cardigan
24	Exile
28	Fifteen
19	I Knew You Were Trouble
34	Look What You Made Me Do
38	Love Story
44	Mean
51	Mine
56	The 1
62	Our Song
66	Picture to Burn
70	...Ready for It?
75	Safe & Sound
78	Shake It Off
82	Should've Said No
86	Teardrops on My Guitar
90	22
95	We Are Never Ever Getting Back Together
100	White Horse
112	Wildest Dreams
105	You Belong with Me

Back to December

Words and Music by Taylor Swift

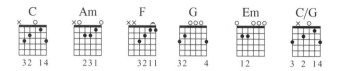

*Capo II

Strum Pattern: 1
Pick Pattern: 5

Intro
Moderately, in 2

*Optional: To match recording, place capo at 2nd fret.

**Ukulele arr. for gtr., next 5 meas.

Verse

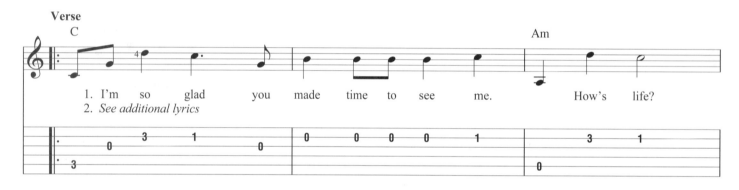

1. I'm so glad you made time to see me. How's life?
2. *See additional lyrics*

Tell me, how's your fam - 'ly? I have - n't seen ____ them in ____ a

while. _____ You've been good,

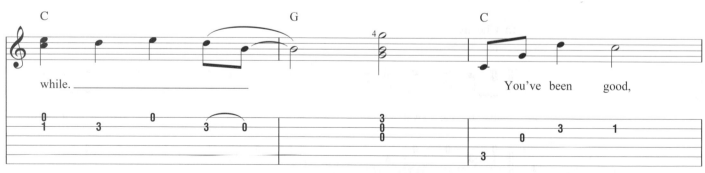

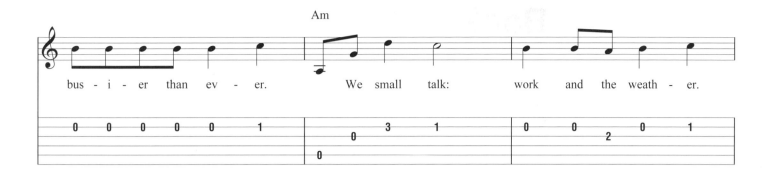

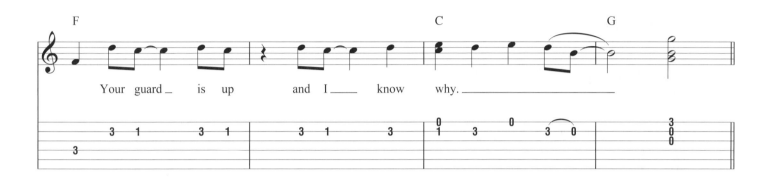

Pre-Chorus

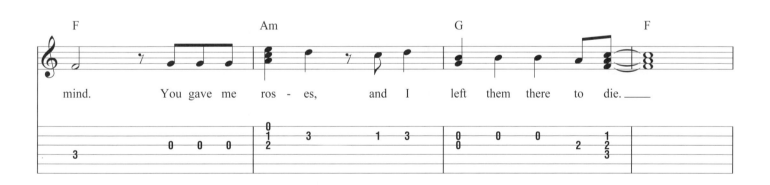

𝄋 Chorus

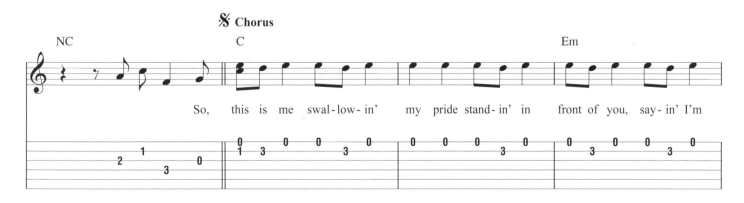

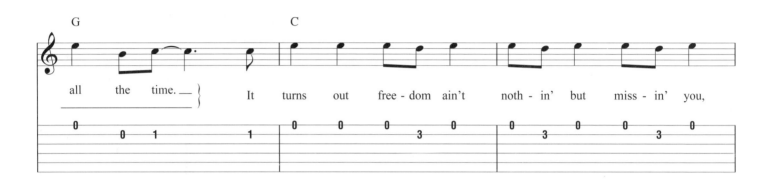

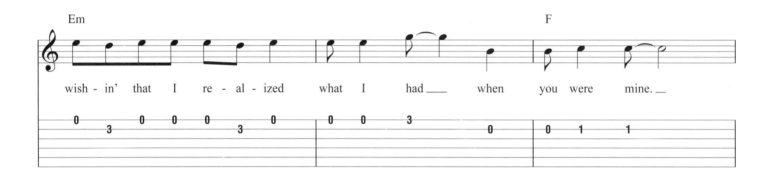

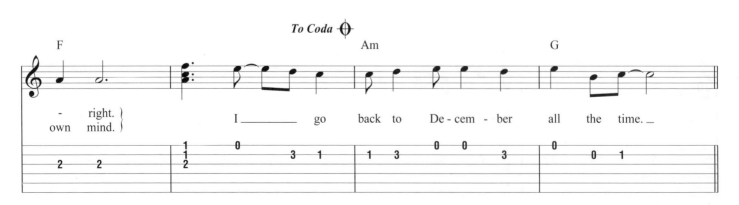

Interlude

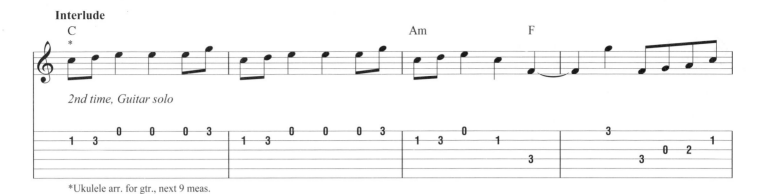

2nd time, Guitar solo

*Ukulele arr. for gtr., next 9 meas.

I miss __ your

Bridge

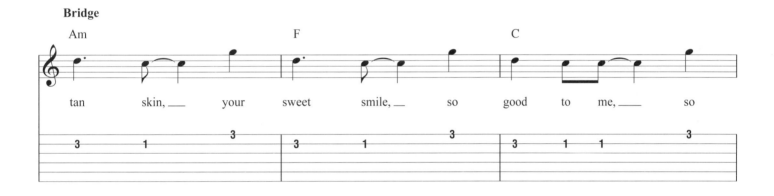

tan skin, __ your sweet smile, __ so good to me, __ so

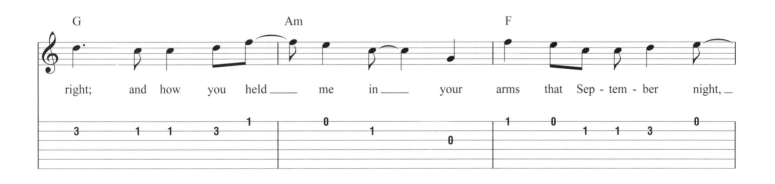

right; and how you held ___ me in ___ your arms that Sep - tem - ber night, __

__ the first time you ev - er saw __ me cry. May - be this is wish - ful think - in',

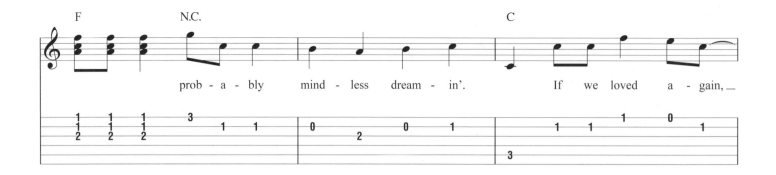

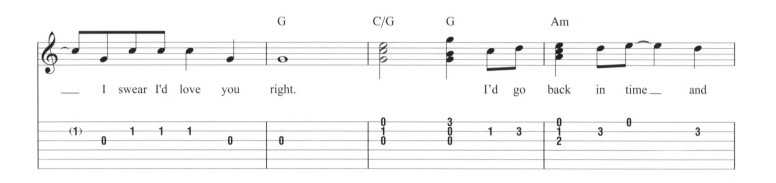

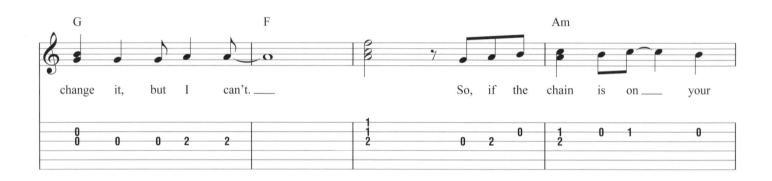

D.S. al Coda

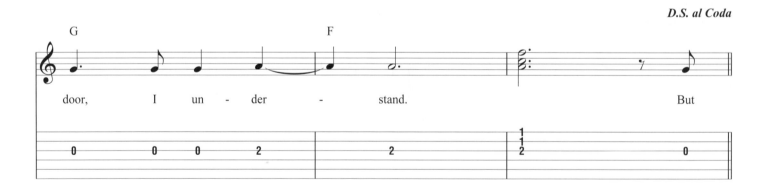

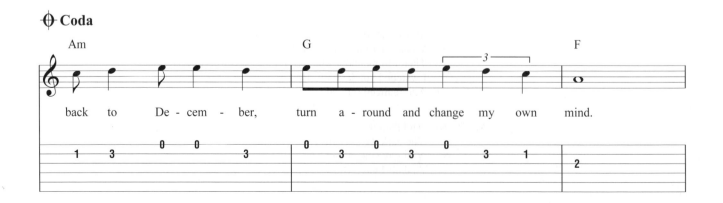

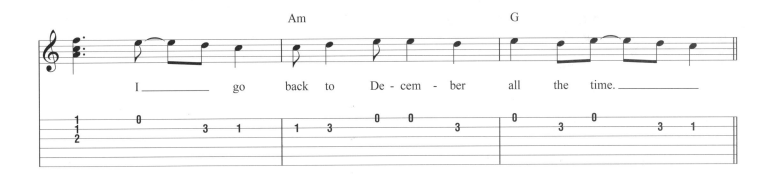

Am   G

I _____ go back to De - cem - ber all the time. _____

Outro

*Ukulele arr. for gtr., next 6 meas.

All the time. ___

**Tie into beat 1 on repeat.

Additional Lyrics

2. These days, I haven't been sleepin';
    Stayin' up, playin' back myself leavin',
    When your birthday passed and I didn't call.
    Then I think about summer, all the beautiful times,
    I watched you laughin' from the passenger side
    And realized I loved you in the fall.

Pre-Chorus   And then the cold came,
    The dark days when fear crept into my mind.
    You gave me all your love,
    And all I gave you was goodbye.

Blank Space

Words and Music by Taylor Swift, Max Martin and Shellback

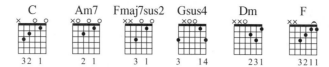

*Capo V

Strum Pattern: 6
Pick Pattern: 4

Intro
Moderately slow

*Optional: To match recording, place capo at 5th fret.

Verse

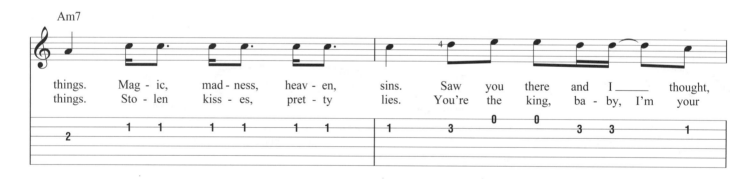

1. Nice to meet you, where you been? I could show you incredible things. Magic, madness, heaven, sins. Saw you there and I _____ thought,
2. Cherry lips, crystal skies, I could show you incredible things. Stolen kisses, pretty lies. You're the king, baby, I'm your

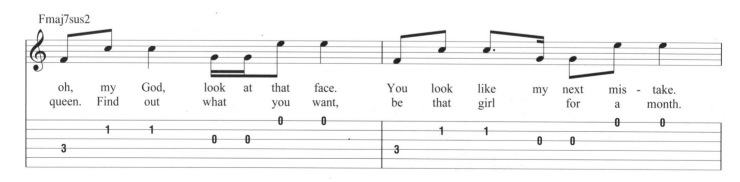

oh, my God, look at that face. You look like my next mistake.
queen. Find out what you want, be that girl for a month.

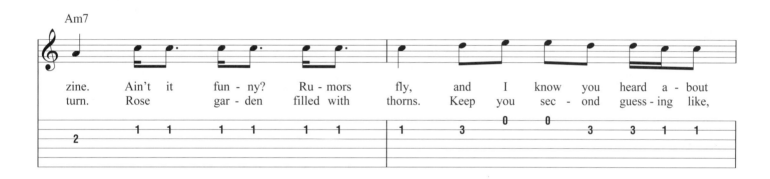

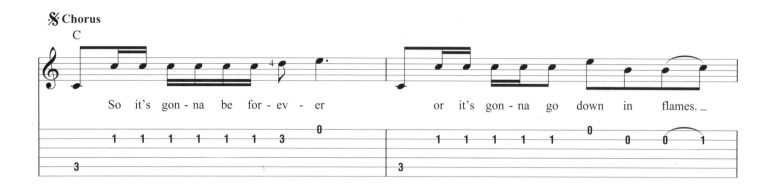

So it's gon - na be for - ev - er or it's gon - na go down in flames. __

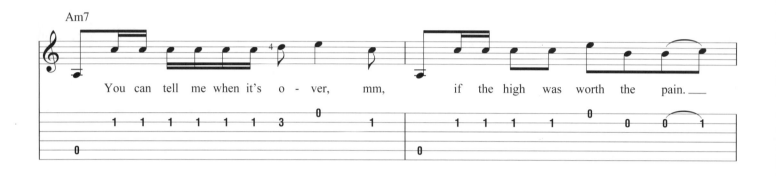

You can tell me when it's o - ver, mm, if the high was worth the pain. __

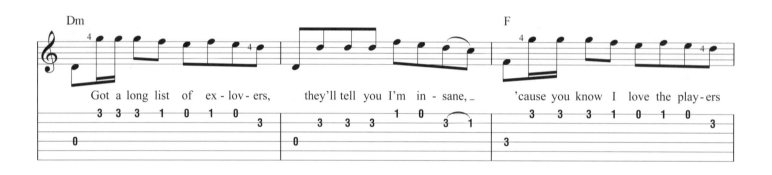

Got a long list of ex - lov - ers, they'll tell you I'm in - sane, __ 'cause you know I love the play - ers

and you love the game. 'Cause we're young and we're reck - less,

we'll take this way too far. __ It -'ll leave you breath - less, mm, or with a nas - ty scar. __

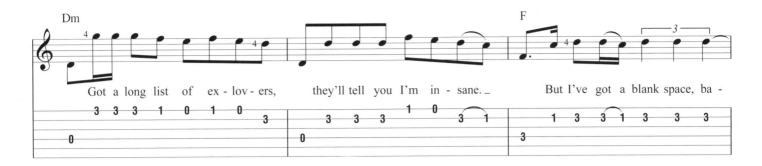

Dm

Got a long list of ex - lov - ers, they'll tell you I'm in - sane. But I've got a blank space, ba -

F

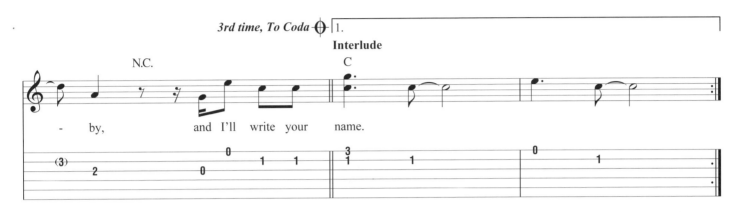

3rd time, To Coda ⊕ ⌐1.

Interlude

N.C.   C

- by,   and I'll write your   name.

⌐2.

Bridge

N.C.

name. Boys   on - ly   want   love   if it's   tor - ture.   Don't   say   I   did - n't,

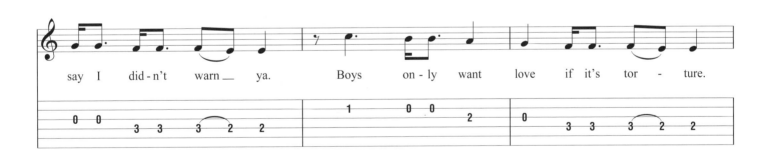

say   I   did - n't   warn   ya.   Boys   on - ly   want   love   if it's   tor - ture.

D.S. al Coda   ⊕ **Coda**

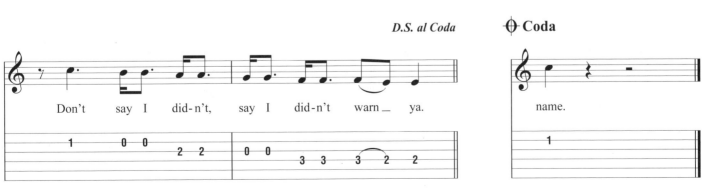

Don't   say   I   did - n't,   say   I   did - n't   warn   ya.   name.

Cardigan

Words and Music by Taylor Swift and Aaron Dessner

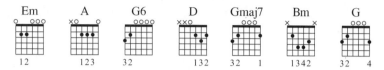

*Capo I

Strum Pattern: 1
Pick Pattern: 5

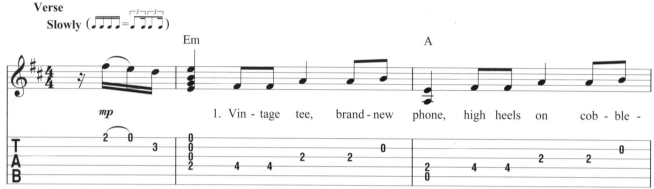

*Optional: To match recording, place capo at 1st fret.

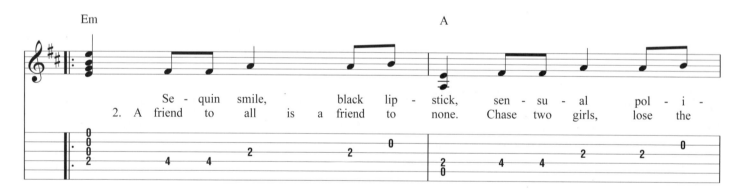

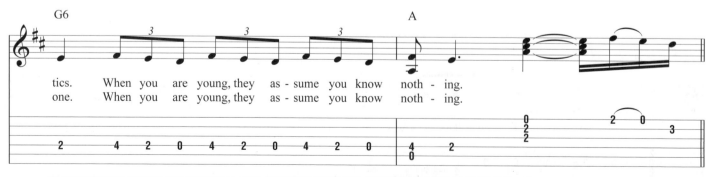

Chorus

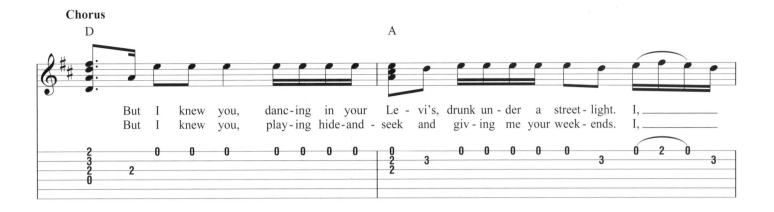

But I knew you, danc-ing in your Le - vi's, drunk un - der a street - light. I,_____
But I knew you, play-ing hide-and - seek and giv - ing me your week - ends. I,_____

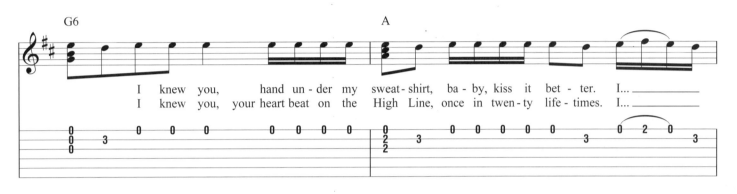

I knew you, hand un - der my sweat - shirt, ba - by, kiss it bet - ter. I..._____
I knew you, your heart beat on the High Line, once in twen - ty life - times. I..._____

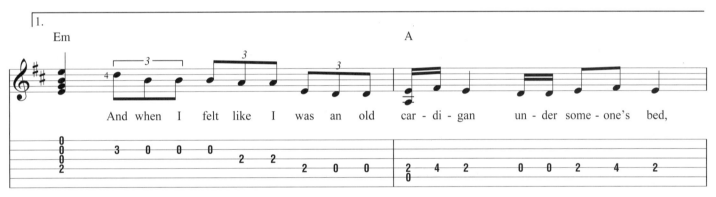

1.

And when I felt like I was an old car - di - gan un - der some - one's bed,

you put me on and said I was your fa - v'rite.

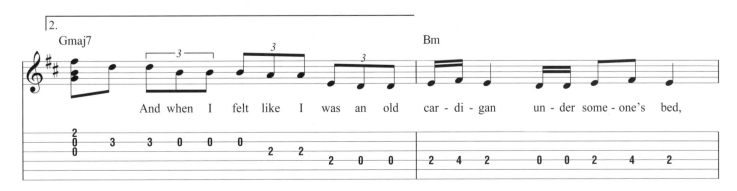

2.

And when I felt like I was an old car - di - gan un - der some - one's bed,

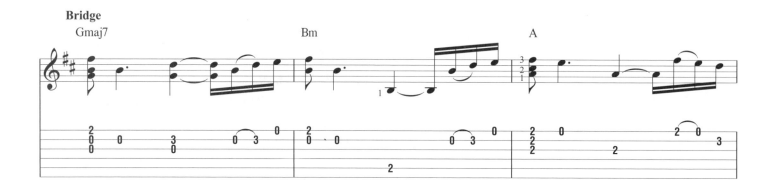

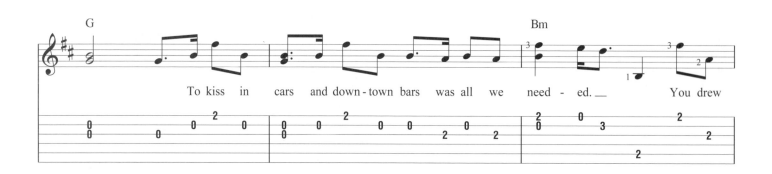

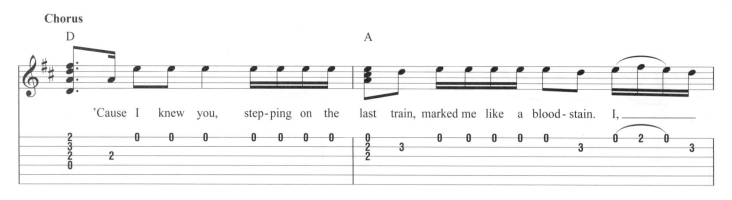

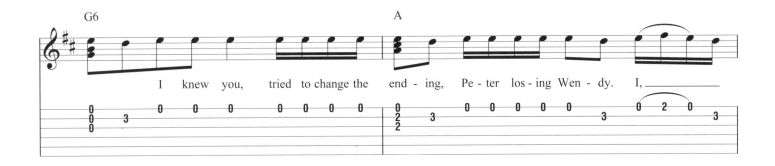

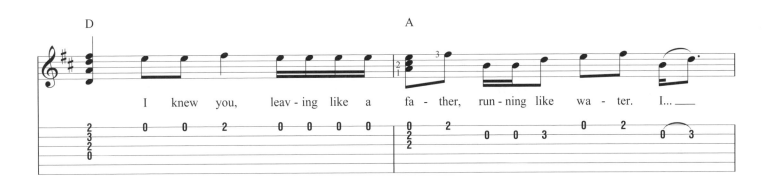

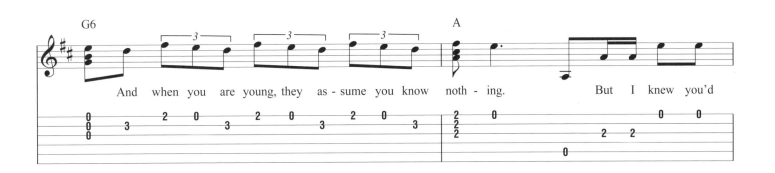

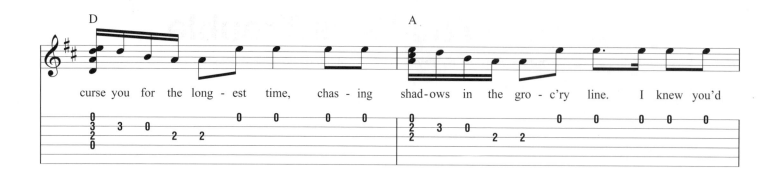

curse you for the long - est time, chas - ing shad-ows in the gro - c'ry line. I knew you'd

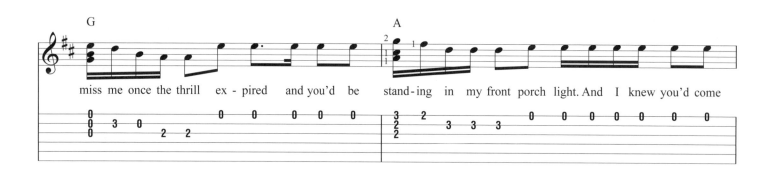

miss me once the thrill ex - pired and you'd be stand-ing in my front porch light. And I knew you'd come

back to me, you'd come back to me. And you'd come back to me, and you'd come

back. And when I felt like I was an old

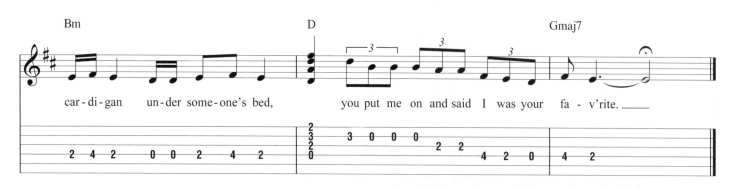

car - di - gan un - der some-one's bed, you put me on and said I was your fa - v'rite. _____

I Knew You Were Trouble

Words and Music by Taylor Swift, Shellback and Max Martin

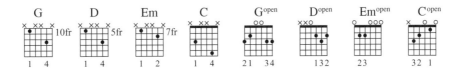

*Tune down 1/2 step:
(low to high) Eb-Ab-Db-Gb-Bb-Eb

Strum Pattern: 6
Pick Pattern: 6

Intro
Fast

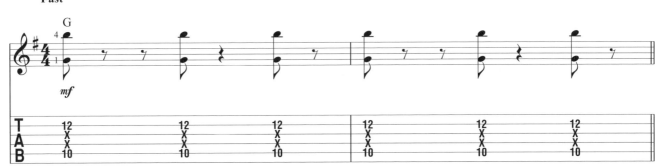

*Optional: To match recording, tune down 1/2 step.

Verse

1. Once up-on a time a few mis-takes a-go, I was in your sights,
2. No a-pol-o-gies, he'll nev-er see you cry. Pre-tends he does-n't know that

**Sung one octave higher throughout.

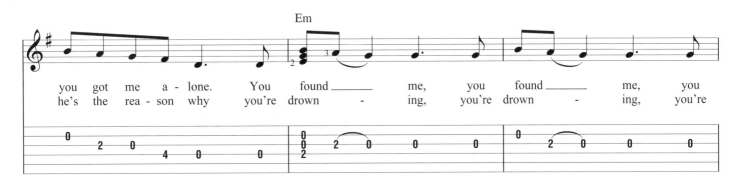

you got me a-lone. You found _____ me, you found _____ me, you
he's the rea-son why you're drown - ing, you're drown - ing, you're

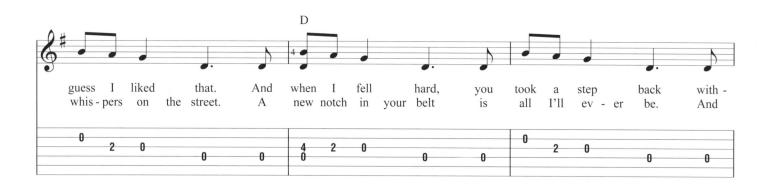

Pre-Chorus

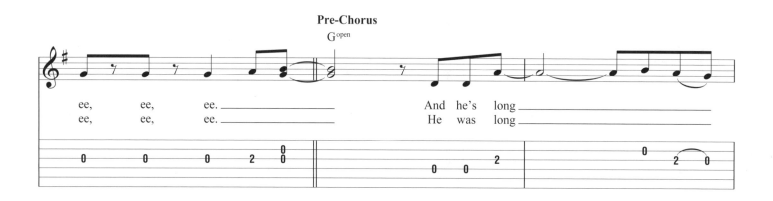

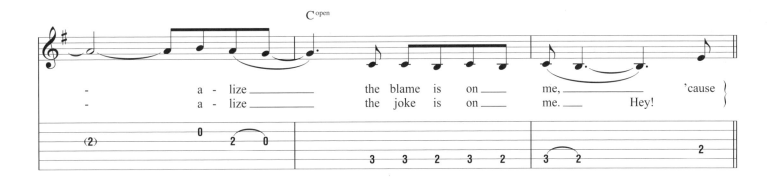

- a - lize _____ the blame is on _____ me, _____ 'cause
- a - lize _____ the joke is on _____ me. Hey!

𝄋 Chorus

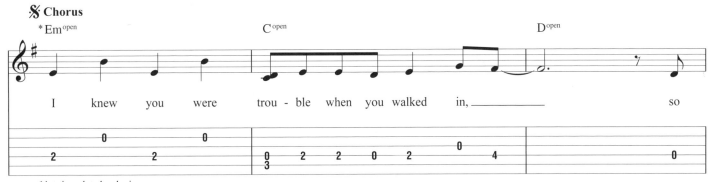

I knew you were trou - ble when you walked in, _____ so

*1st time, let chords ring.
2nd & 3rd times, **Half-time feel**.

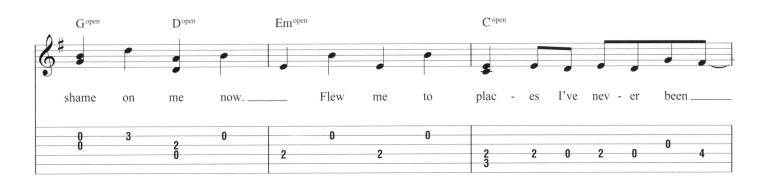

shame on me now. _____ Flew me to plac - es I've nev - er been _____

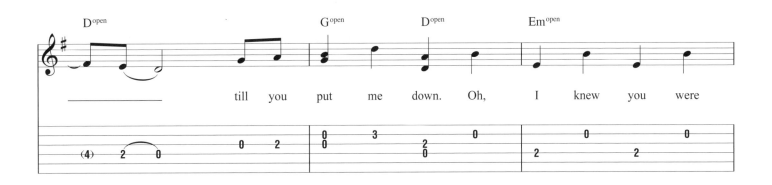

_____ till you put me down. Oh, I knew you were

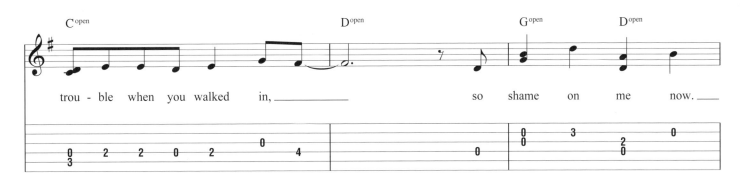

trou - ble when you walked in, _____ so shame on me now. _____

Flew me to plac - es I've nev - er been. _____ Now I'm

ly - ing on the cold, ___ hard ___ ground. Oh, _____ oh, ___

*2nd & 3rd times, substitute chords in parentheses.

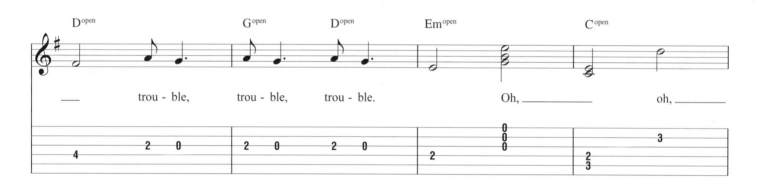

___ trou - ble, trou - ble, trou - ble. Oh, ___ oh, ___

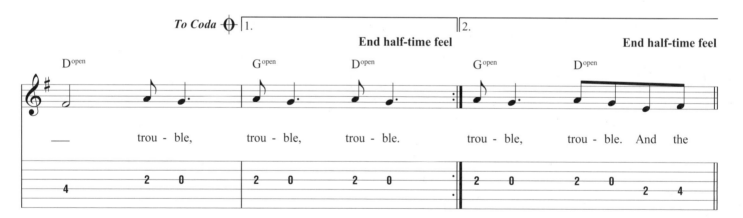

___ trou - ble, trou - ble, trou - ble. trou - ble, trou - ble. And the

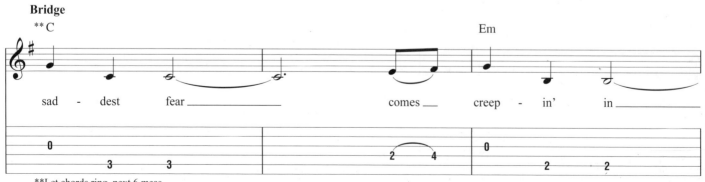

sad - dest fear _____ comes ___ creep - in' in _____

**Let chords ring, next 6 meas.

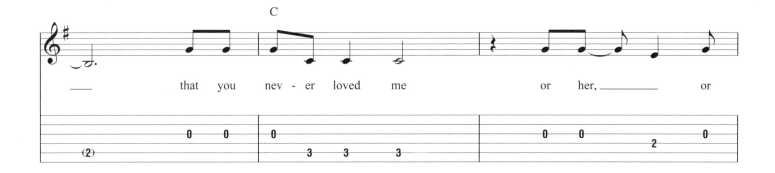

that you nev-er loved me or her, or

D.S. al Coda

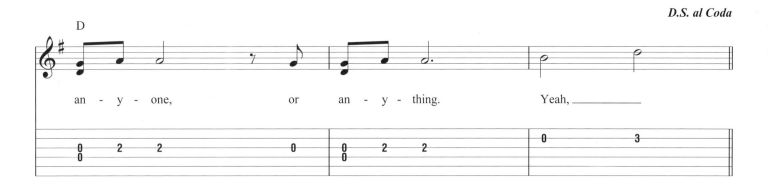

an-y-one, or an-y-thing. Yeah,

⊕ Coda

Outro

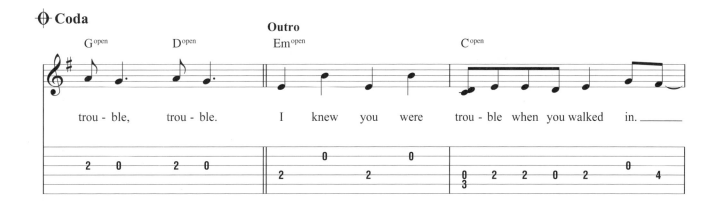

trou-ble, trou-ble. I knew you were trou-ble when you walked in.

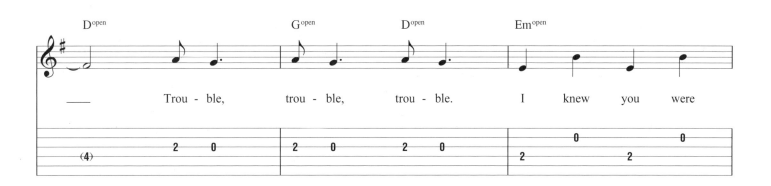

Trou-ble, trou-ble, trou-ble. I knew you were

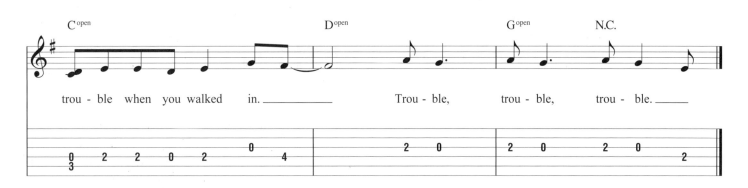

trou-ble when you walked in. Trou-ble, trou-ble, trou-ble.

Exile

Words and Music by Taylor Swift, William Bowery and Justin Vernon

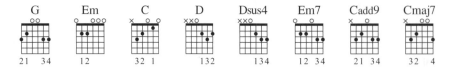

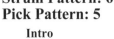

*Tune down 1/2 step:
(low to high) Eb-Ab-Db-Gb-Bb-Eb

Strum Pattern: 6
Pick Pattern: 5

Intro
Slow

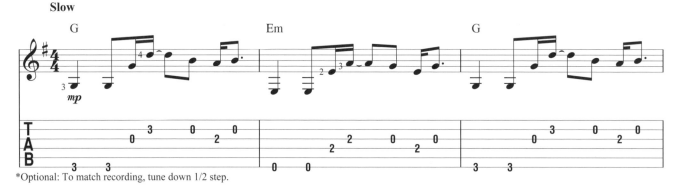

*Optional: To match recording, tune down 1/2 step.

Verse

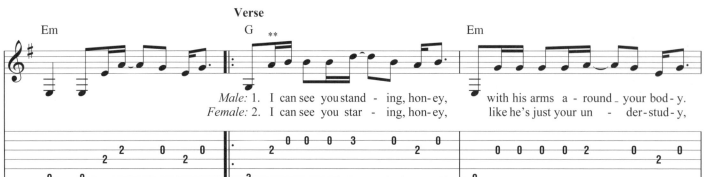

Male: 1. I can see you stand - ing, hon-ey, with his arms a - round _ your bod - y,
Female: 2. I can see you star - ing, hon-ey, like he's just your un - der-stud - y,

**1st time, sung one octave lower, next 16 meas.

Laugh-ing, but the joke's _ not fun - ny at all. ___ And it took you five _ whole min - utes
like you'd get your knuck - les blood-y for me. ___ Sec-ond, third and hun - dredth chanc - es,

to pack us up and leave _ me with it, hold-ing all this love _ out here in the hall. ___
bal-anc-ing on break - ing branch - es, those _ eyes add in - sult to in-ju-ry. ___

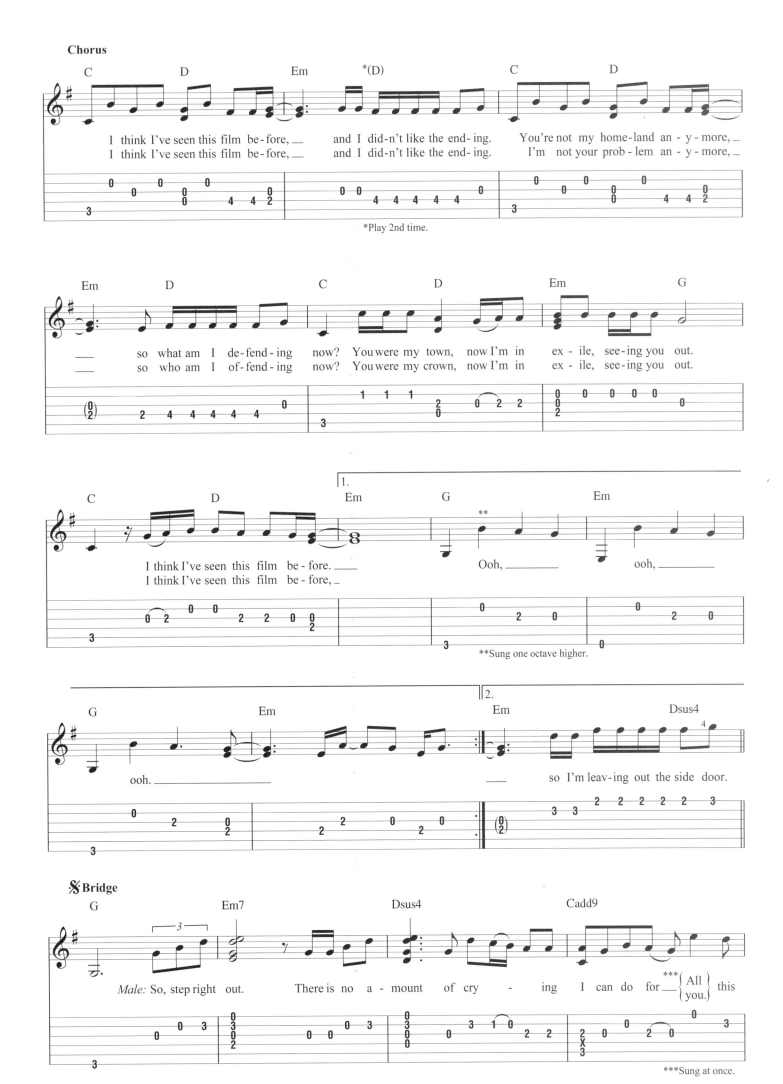

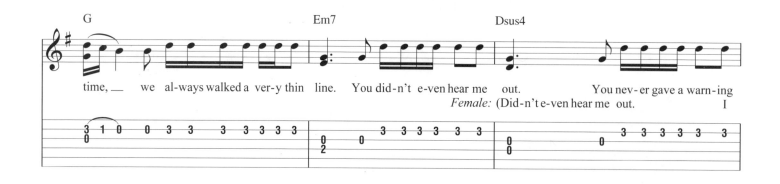

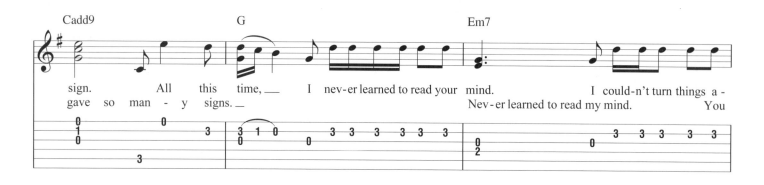

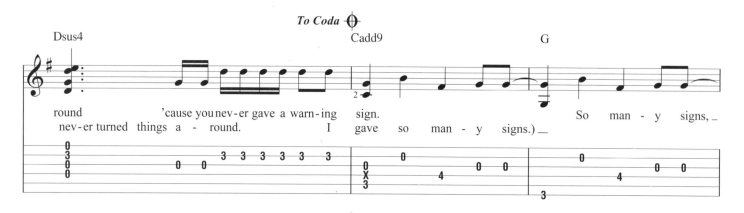

D.S. al Coda

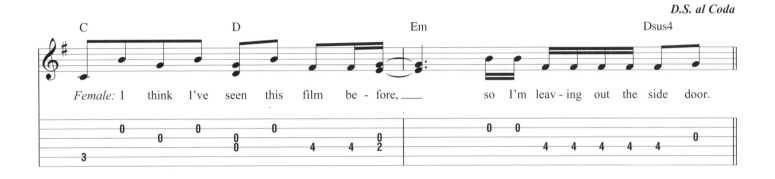

Coda

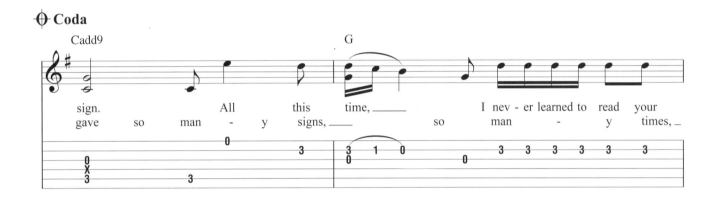

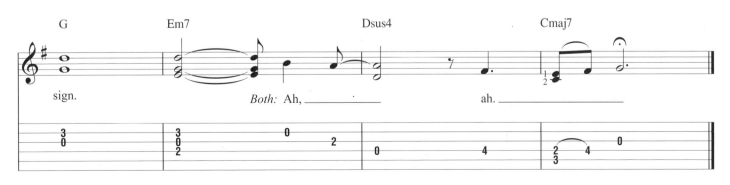

Fifteen

Words and Music by Taylor Swift

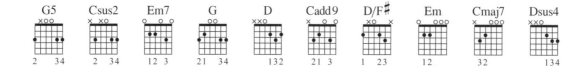

Strum Pattern: 3, 6
Pick Pattern: 2, 5

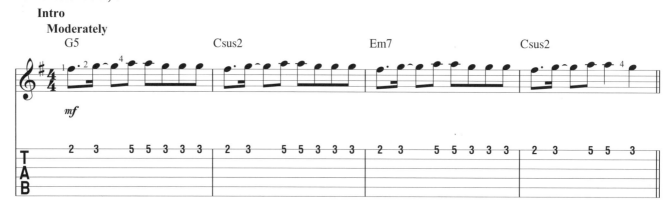

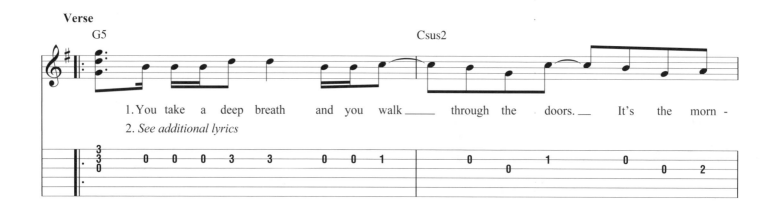

1. You take a deep breath and you walk ____ through the doors. ____ It's the morn-
2. *See additional lyrics*

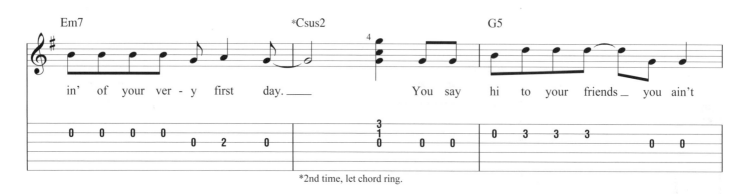

in' of your ver - y first day. ____ You say hi to your friends __ you ain't

*2nd time, let chord ring.

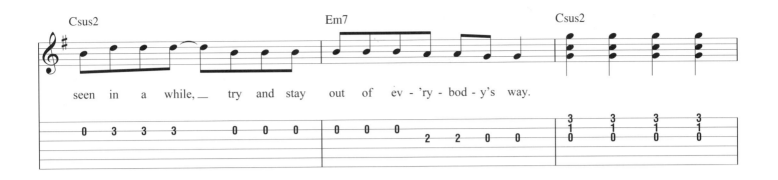

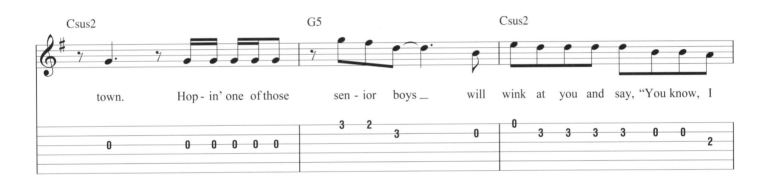

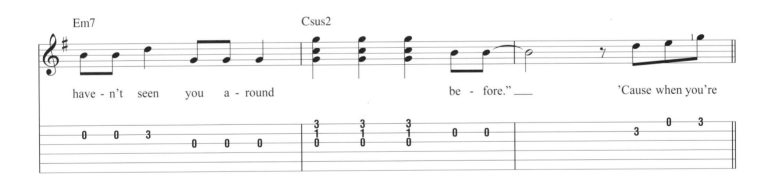

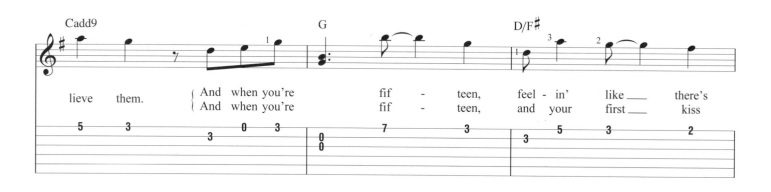

Cadd9   G   D/F#

lieve   them.   And   when   you're   fif - teen,   feel - in'   like _____ there's
                 And   when   you're   fif - teen,   and   your   first _____ kiss

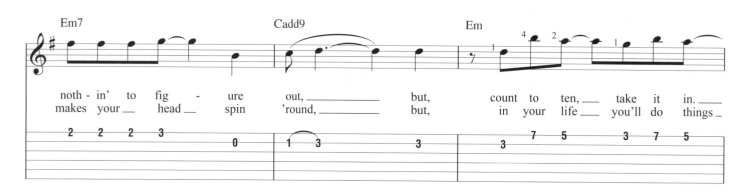

Em7   Cadd9   Em

noth - in'   to   fig - ure   out, _____ but,   count   to   ten, __ take   it   in. __
makes   your __ head __ spin   'round, _____ but,   in   your   life __ you'll   do   things _

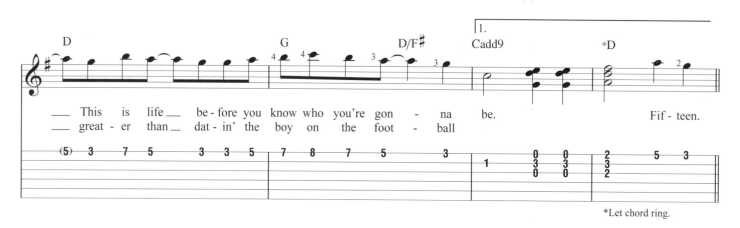

D   G   D/F#   Cadd9   *D

1.

__ This   is   life __ be - fore   you   know   who   you're   gon - na   be.   Fif - teen.
__ great - er   than __ dat - in'   the   boy   on   the   foot - ball

*Let chord ring.

Interlude

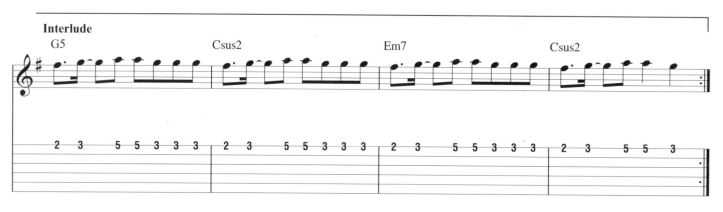

G5   Csus2   Em7   Csus2

2.

Guitar Solo

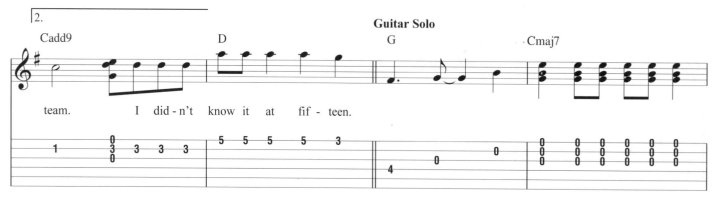

Cadd9   D   G   Cmaj7

team.   I   did - n't   know   it   at   fif - teen.

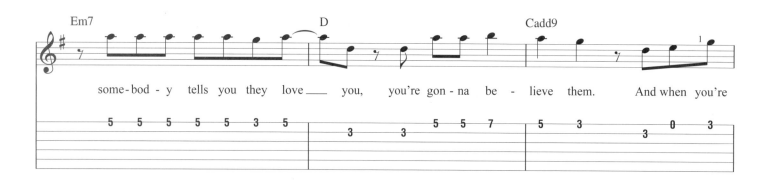

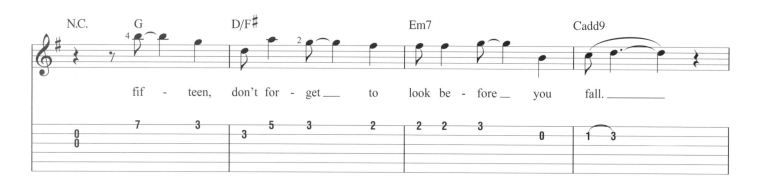

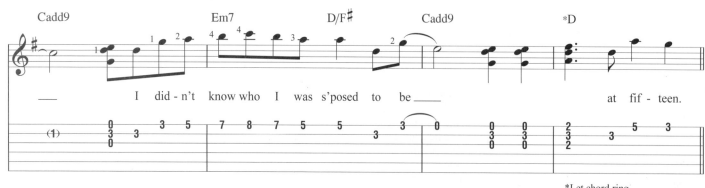

*Let chord ring.

Outro

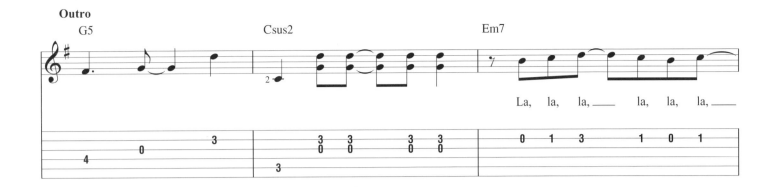

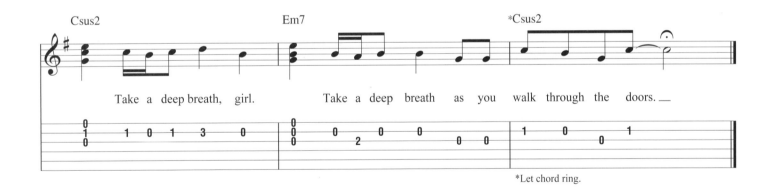

*Let chord ring.

Additional Lyrics

2. You sit in class next to a redhead named Abigail
And soon enough we're best friends,
Laughin' at the other girls who think they're so cool.
We'll be out of here as soon as we can.
And then you're on your very first date
And he's got a car and you're feelin' like flyin'.
And you mama's waitin' up and you're thinkin' he's the one
And you're dancin' 'round your room when the night ends,
When the night ends.

Look What You Made Me Do

Words and Music by Taylor Swift, Jack Antonoff, Richard Fairbrass, Fred Fairbrass and Rob Manzoli

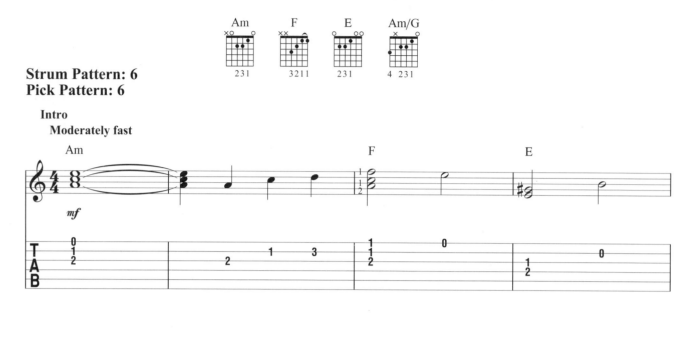

Strum Pattern: 6
Pick Pattern: 6

Intro
Moderately fast

Verse

N.C.(Am)

1. I don't like your lit - tle games, don't like your tilt - ed
3. I don't like your king - dom keys, they, once be - longed to

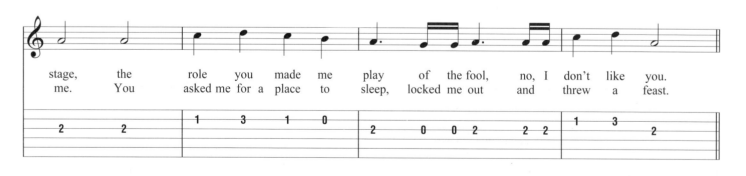

stage, the role you made me play of the fool, no, I don't like you.
me. You asked me for a place to sleep, locked me out and threw a feast.

Verse

N.C.(Am)

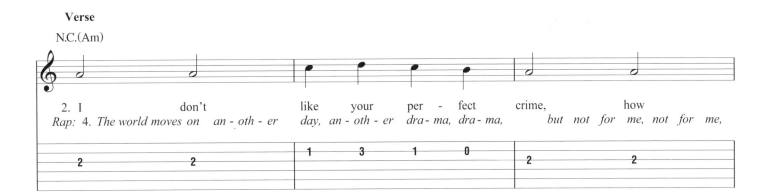

2. I don't like your per - fect crime, how
Rap: 4. The world moves on an - oth - er day, an - oth - er dra - ma, dra - ma, but not for me, not for me,

you laugh when you lie. You said the gun was
all I think a - bout is kar - ma. And then the world moves on, but one thing's for sure:

Pre-Chorus

Am

mine. Is - n't cool. No, I don't like you. But I got smart - er, I got
may - be I got mine but you'll all get yours.

Am/G

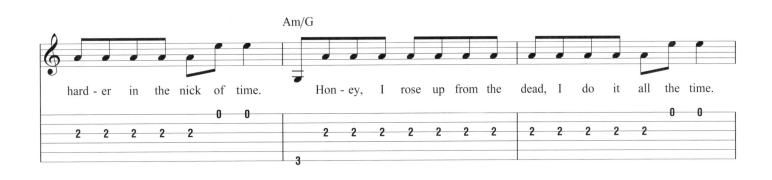

hard - er in the nick of time. Hon - ey, I rose up from the dead, I do it all the time.

F   E

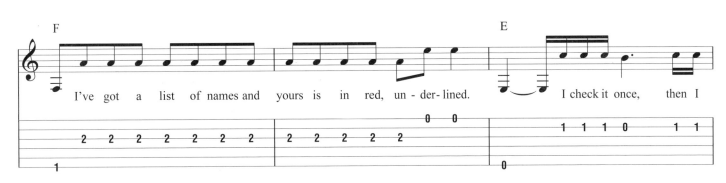

I've got a list of names and yours is in red, un - der- lined. I check it once, then I

Chorus

Am

Spoken: *Half sung:*

check it twice. *Oh!* Ooh, look what you made me do, look what you made me

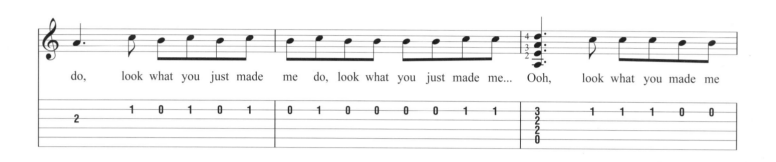

do, look what you just made me do, look what you just made me... Ooh, look what you made me

3rd time, To Coda

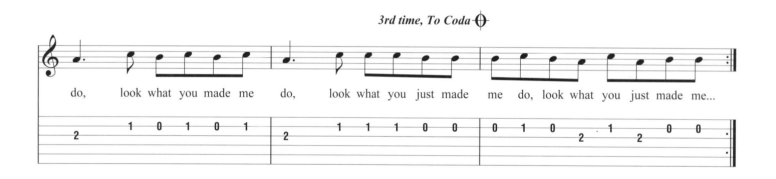

do, look what you made me do, look what you just made me do, look what you just made me...

Bridge

Am   F

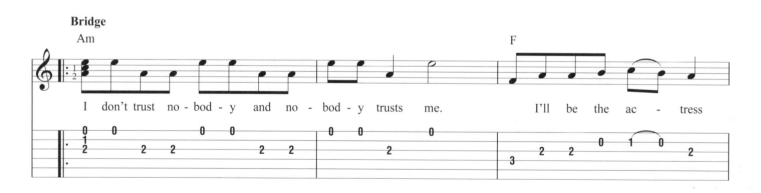

I don't trust no-bod-y and no-bod-y trusts me.   I'll be the ac-tress

1., 2., 3.   *4.*   **Interlude**

E   E   Am

star-ring in your bad dreams.   star-ring in your bad dreams.

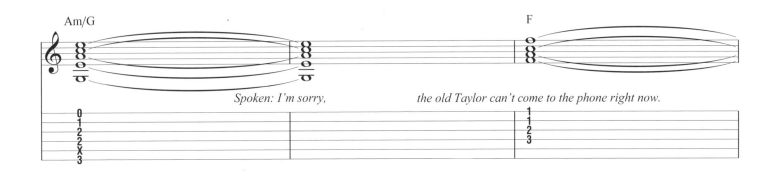

Spoken: I'm sorry, the old Taylor can't come to the phone right now.

D.S. al Coda

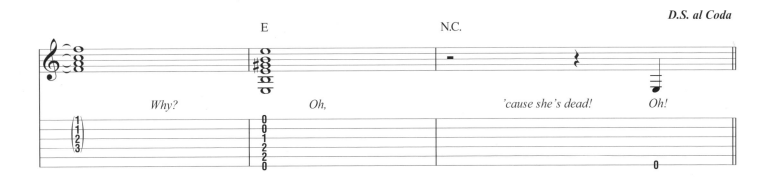

Why? Oh, 'cause she's dead! Oh!

⊕ **Coda**

Outro-Chorus

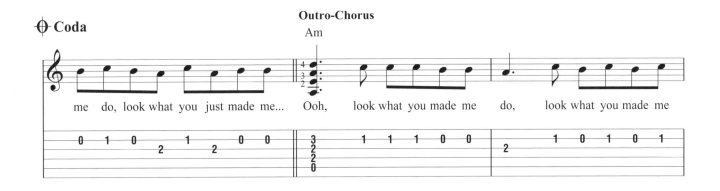

me do, look what you just made me... Ooh, look what you made me do, look what you made me

do, look what you just made me do, look what you just made me... Ooh, look what you made me

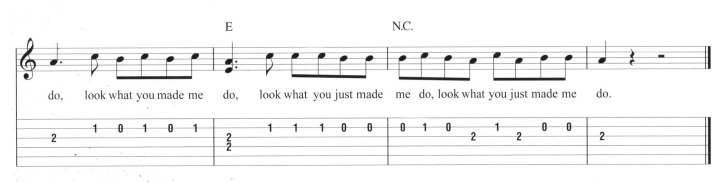

do, look what you made me do, look what you just made me do, look what you just made me do.

Love Story

Words and Music by Taylor Swift

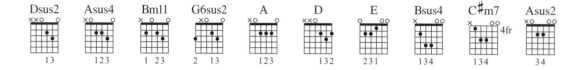

Strum Pattern: 1, 6
Pick Pattern: 4

Intro
Moderately

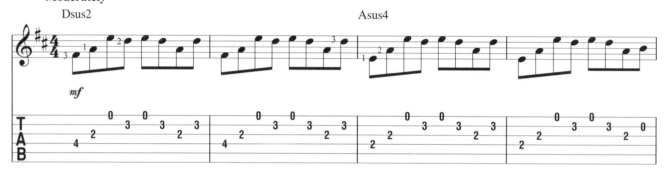

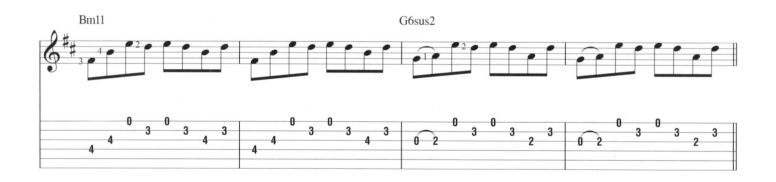

Verse

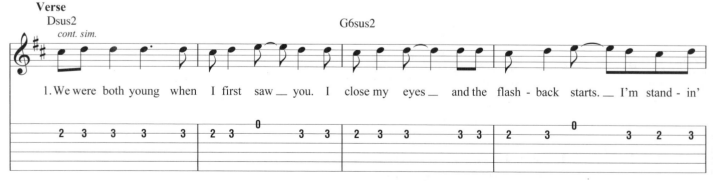

1. We were both young when I first saw __ you. I close my eyes __ and the flash - back starts. __ I'm stand - in'

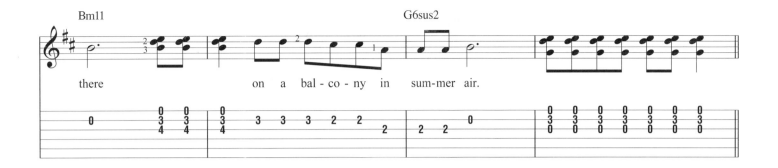

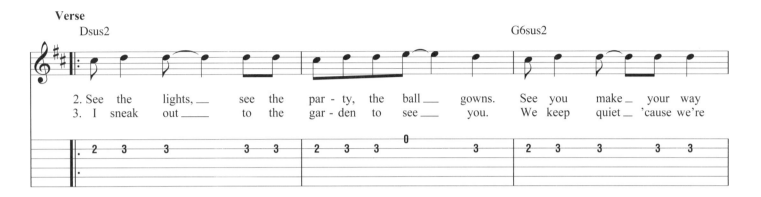

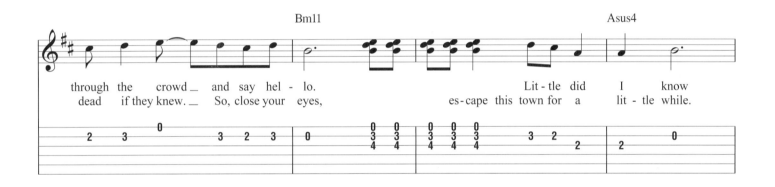

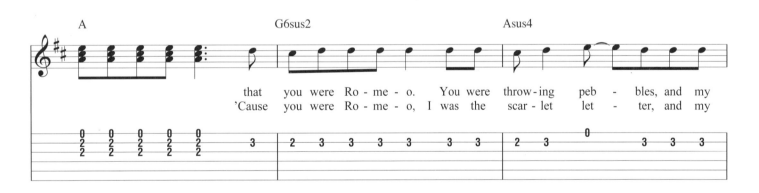

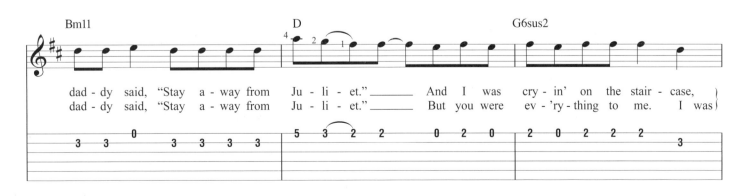

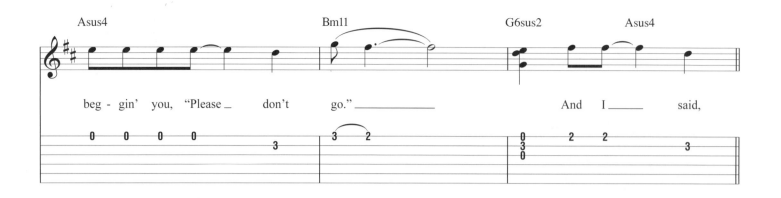

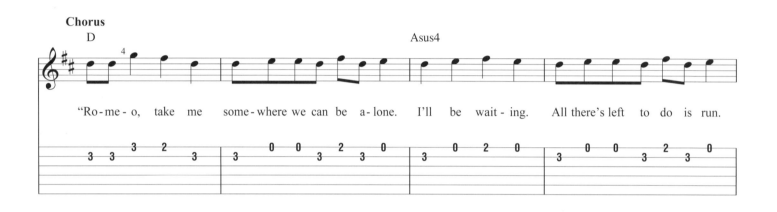

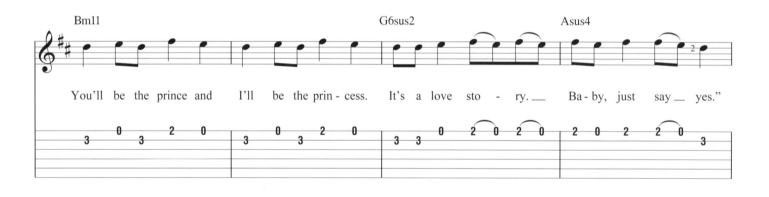

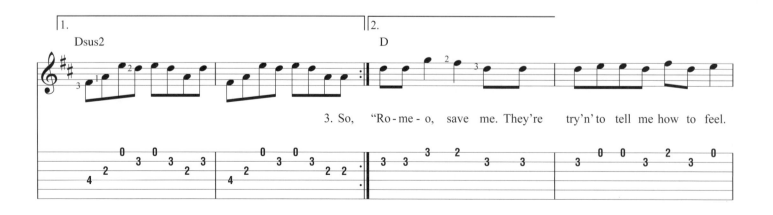

This love is dif - fi - cult, but it's __ real. __ Don't be a - fraid. We'll make it out of this mess.

Interlude

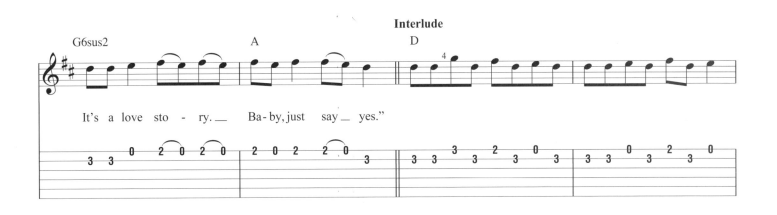

It's a love sto - ry. __ Ba - by, just say __ yes."

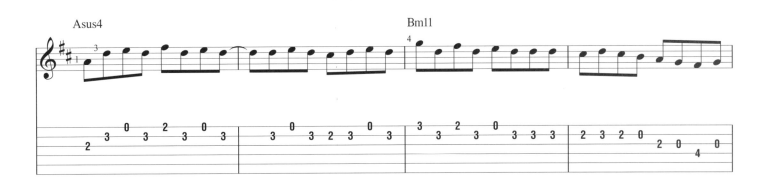

Bridge

I got tired of wait - ing. __ won - der - in' if

*Let chords ring throughout Bridge.

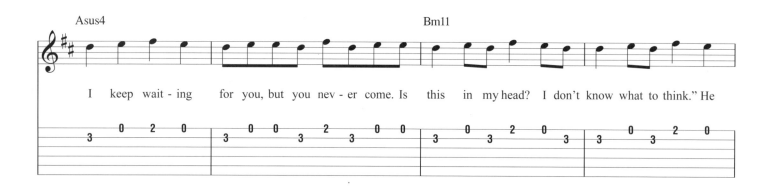

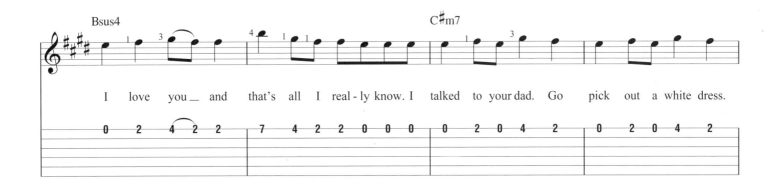

I love you — and that's all I real- ly know. I talked to your dad. Go pick out a white dress.

Outro

It's a love sto - ry. — Ba - by, just say — yes." Oh, — oh, oh, —

—— oh, — oh, oh, —— oh. 'Cause

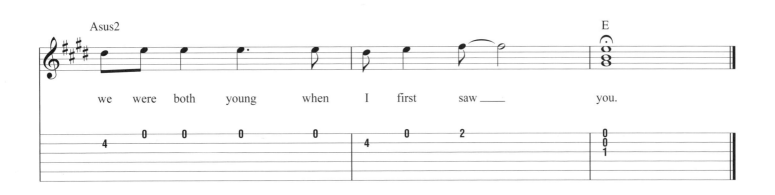

we were both young when I first saw — you.

Mean

Words and Music by Taylor Swift

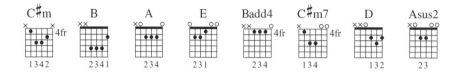

Strum Pattern: 2, 5
Pick Pattern: 1, 4

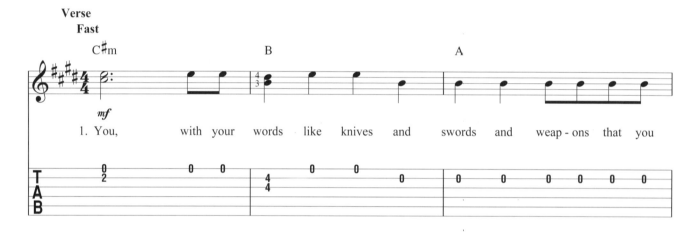

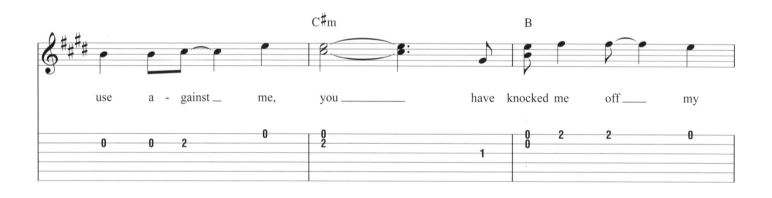

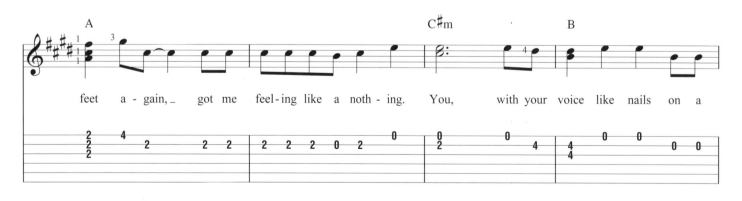

chalk - board, call - ing me out ___ when I'm wound - ed. You, pick - ing on the weak - er man. ___

Pre-Chorus

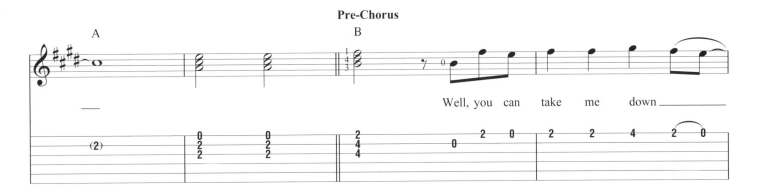

Well, you can take me down _____

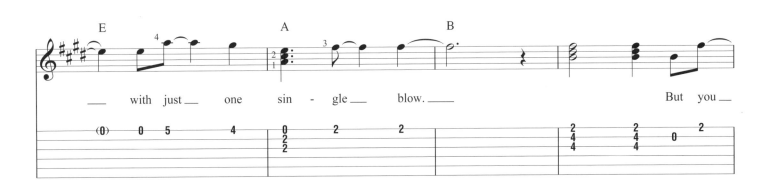

___ with just ___ one sin - gle ___ blow. ___ But you ___

𝄉 **Chorus**

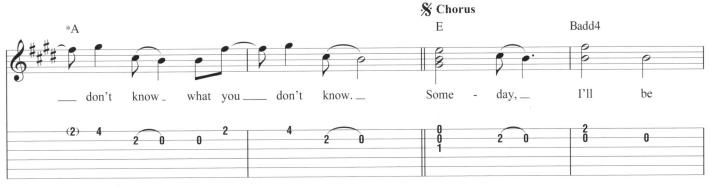

___ don't know ___ what you ___ don't know. ___ Some - day, ___ I'll be

*Let chord ring.

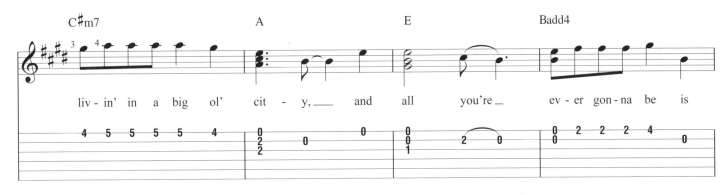

liv - in' in a big ol' cit - y, ___ and all you're ___ ev - er gon - na be is

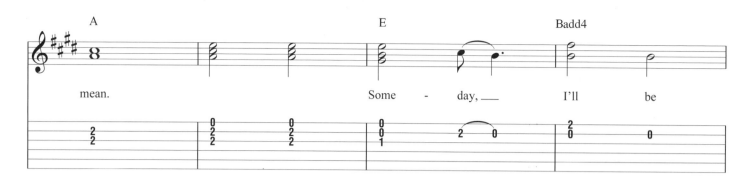

mean. Some - day, ___ I'll be

big e-nough so you can't hit me, ___ and all you're ev - er gon - na be is

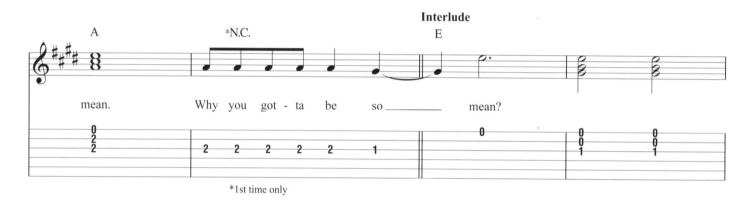

mean. Why you got - ta be so _____ mean?

*1st time only

To Coda ⊕

Verse

2. You, with your switch - ing sides and your

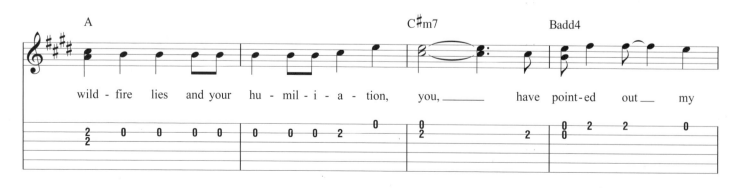

wild - fire lies and your hu - mil - i - a - tion, you, _____ have point - ed out ___ my

flaws a - gain, _ as if I don't al - read - y see them.   I walk with my _ head down, _ try'n' to

block you out 'cause I'll nev - er im - press you.   I   just wan - na feel _ o -

Interlude

kay a - gain. _   I'll bet   you got   pushed a - round, _____

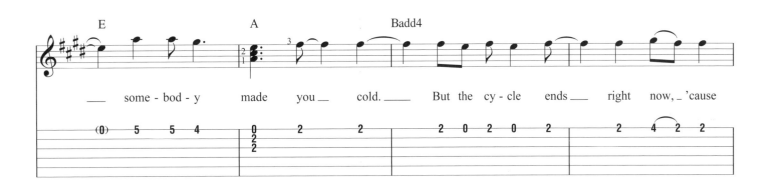

_ some - bod - y   made   you _ cold. _ But the cy - cle ends _ right   now, _ 'cause

D.S. al Coda

you can't lead _ me down _ that road _ and you _ don't know _ what you _ don't know. _

Coda

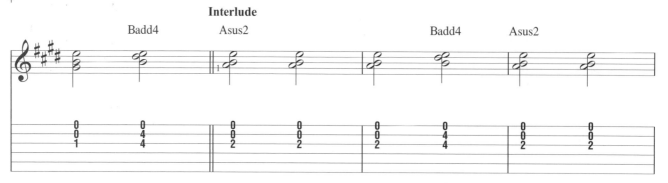

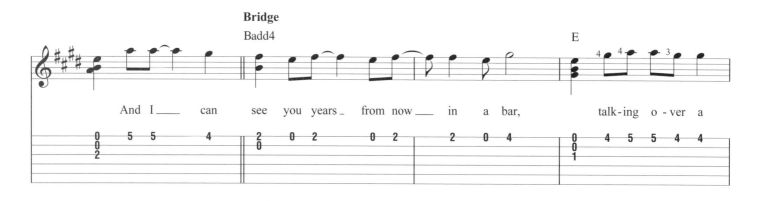

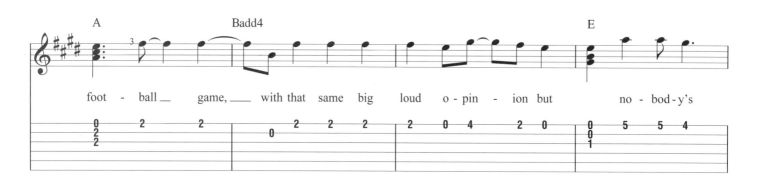

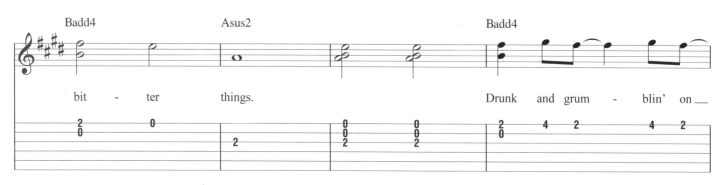

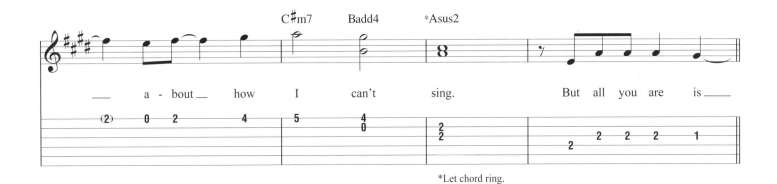

C#m7   Badd4   *Asus2

___ a - bout ___ how I can't sing. But all you are is ___

*Let chord ring.

Interlude

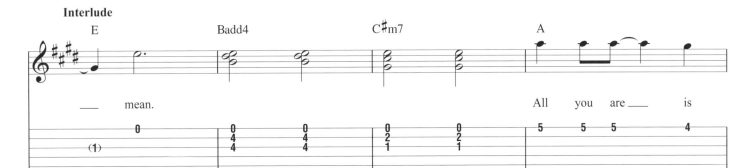

E   Badd4   C#m7   A

___ mean.   All you are ___ is

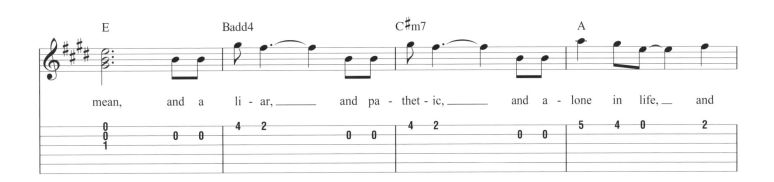

E   Badd4   C#m7   A

mean,   and a li - ar, ___ and pa - thet - ic, ___ and a - lone in life, ___ and

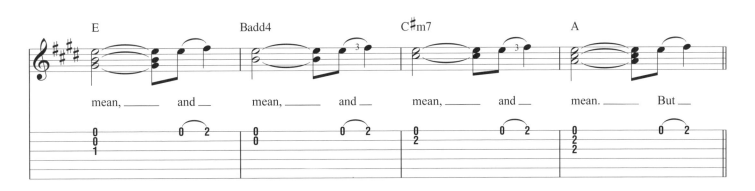

E   Badd4   C#m7   A

mean, ___ and ___ mean, ___ and ___ mean, ___ and ___ mean. ___ But ___

Chorus

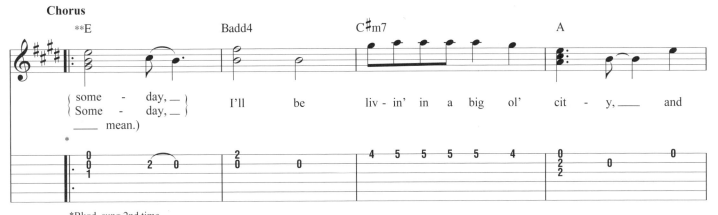

**E   Badd4   C#m7   A

{ some - day, ___ }
{ Some - day, ___ }
{ ___ mean.) }

I'll be liv - in' in a big ol' cit - y, ___ and

*Bkgd. sung 2nd time.
**1st time, N.C., next 8 meas.

49

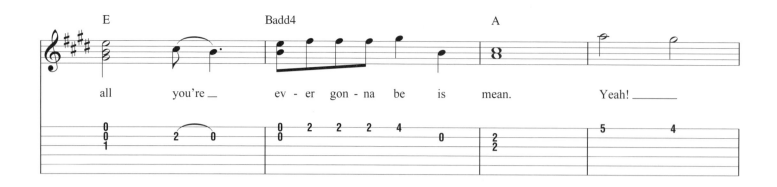

all you're __ ev - er gon - na be is mean. Yeah! _____

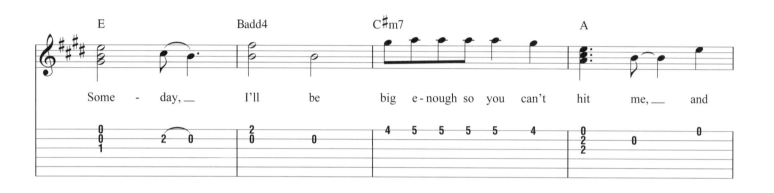

Some - day, __ I'll be big e - nough so you can't hit me, __ and

1.

all you're ev - er gon - na be is mean.

(Why you got - ta be so __

*2nd time, let chords ring till end.

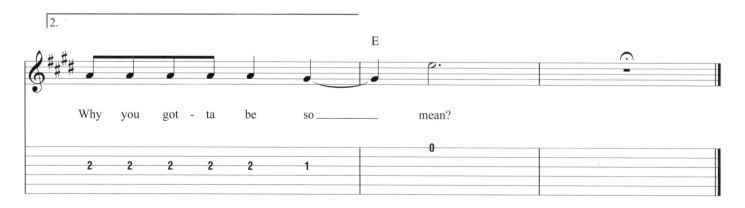

2.

Why you got - ta be so _____ mean?

Mine

Words and Music by Taylor Swift

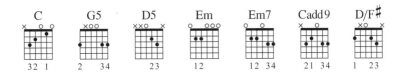

Strum Pattern: 1, 3
Pick Pattern: 3

Ah, ah, ___ ah. ___

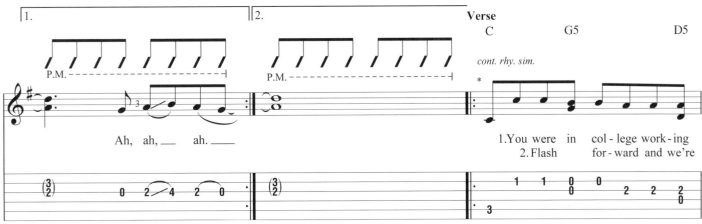

Ah, ah, ___ ah. ___

1.You were in col-lege work-ing
2.Flash for-ward and we're

*Sung as written throughout Verse.

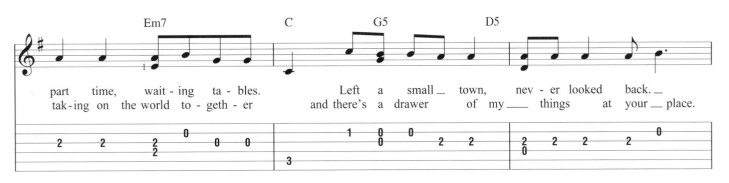

part time, wait-ing ta-bles.   Left a small ___ town, nev-er looked back. ___
tak-ing on the world to-geth-er   and there's a drawer of my ___ things at your ___ place.

I was a flight___ risk with a fear of fall - ing,
You learn my se - crets and you fig - ure out why I'm guard - ed.

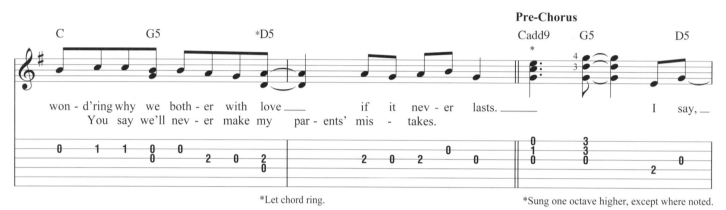

Pre-Chorus

won - d'ring why we both - er with love ___ if it nev - er lasts. ___ I say, ___
You say we'll nev - er make my par - ents' mis - takes.

*Let chord ring.

*Sung one octave higher, except where noted.

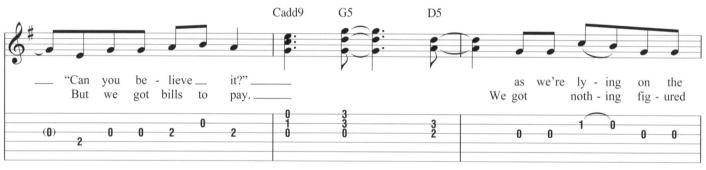

___ "Can you be - lieve___ it?" ___ as we're ly - ing on the
But we got bills to pay. ___ We got noth - ing fig - ured

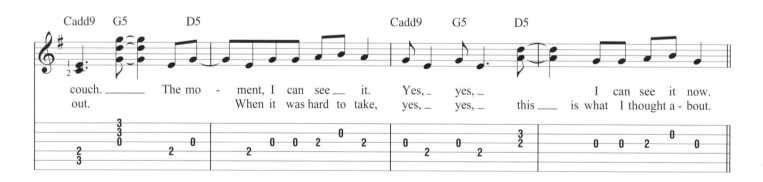

couch. ___ The mo - ment, I can see___ it. Yes,_ yes,_ I can see it now.
out. When it was hard to take, yes,_ yes,_ this___ is what I thought a - bout.

𝄋 Chorus

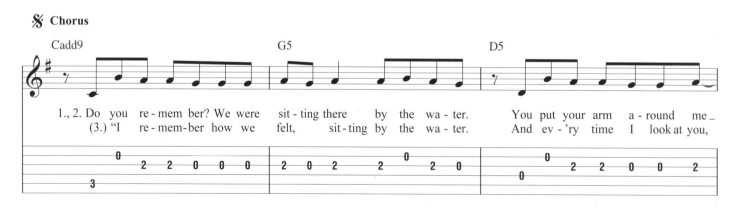

1., 2. Do you re - mem - ber? We were sit - ting there by the wa - ter. You put your arm a - round me_
(3.) "I re - mem - ber how we felt, sit - ting by the wa - ter. And ev - 'ry time I look at you,

*Bkgd vocals sung 2nd time only.

Interlude

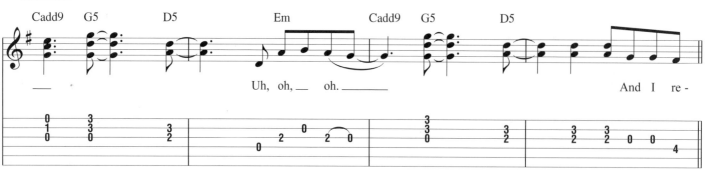

Uh, oh, __ oh. And I re-

Bridge

mem - ber that fight, two - thir - ty A. M. You said ev - 'ry - thing was slip - ping right

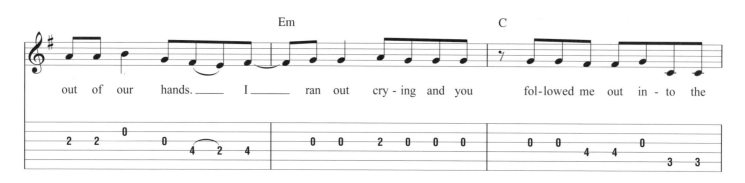

out of our hands. __ I __ ran out cry - ing and you fol - lowed me out in - to the

Pre-Chorus

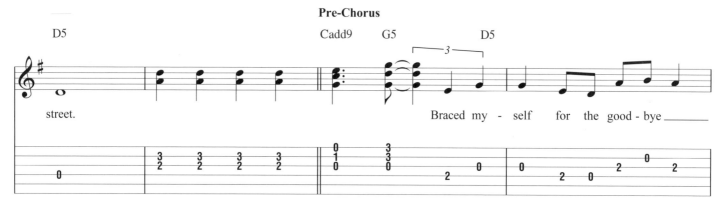

street. Braced my - self for the good - bye __

'cause that's all __ I've ev - er known. __ And you __

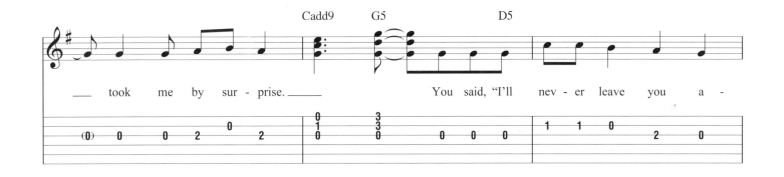

took me by sur - prise. _____ You said, "I'll nev - er leave you a -

D.S. al Coda
(take 2nd ending)

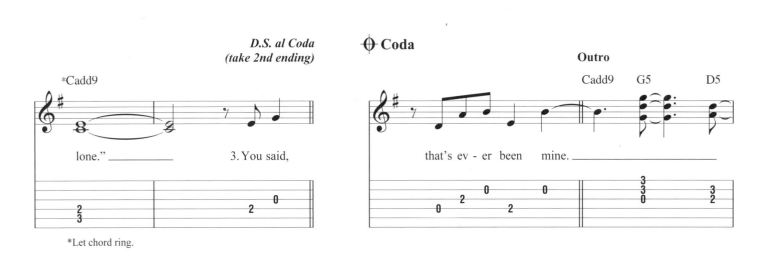

lone." _____ 3. You said,

*Let chord ring.

⊕ Coda

Outro

that's ev - er been mine. _____

Do you be - lieve it? We're gon - na make it, now.

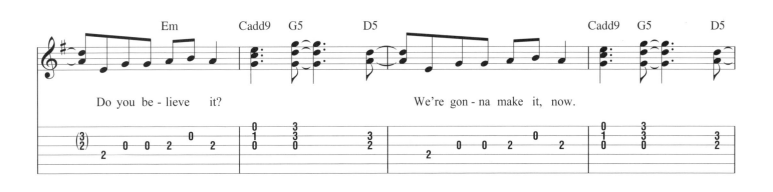

And I can see ___ it. I can see it now.

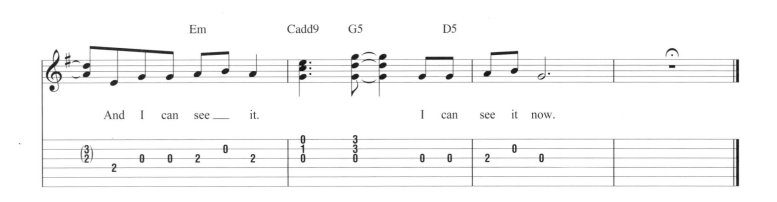

The 1

Words and Music by Taylor Swift and Aaron Dessner

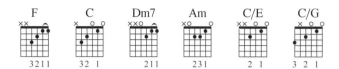

Strum Pattern: 2
Pick Pattern: 5

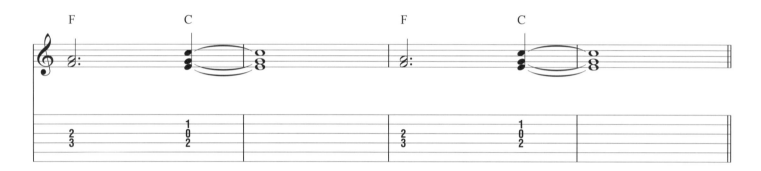

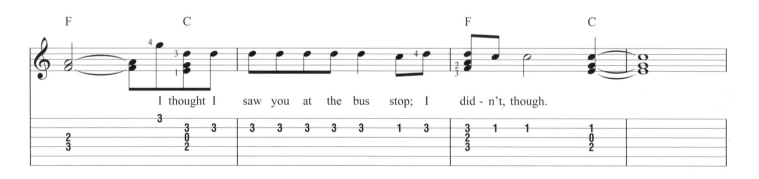

1. I'm do-ing good; I'm on some new shit. Been say-ing yes in-stead of no.

I thought I saw you at the bus stop; I did-n't, though.

Chorus

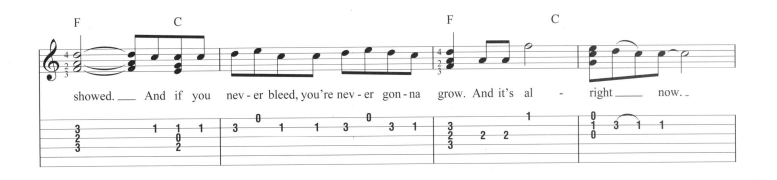

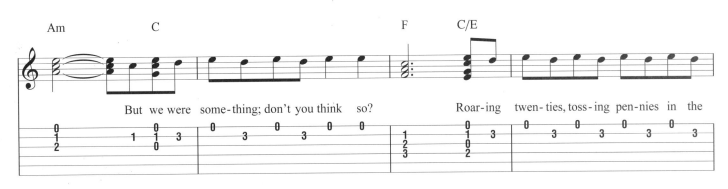

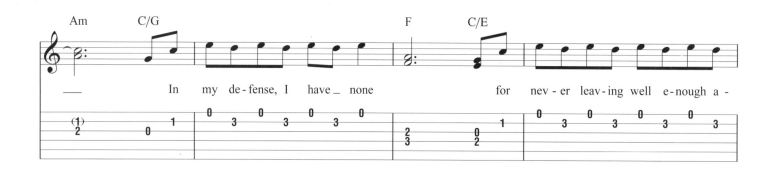

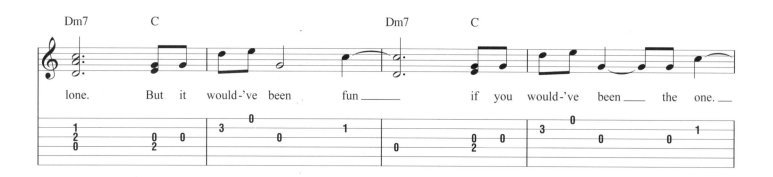

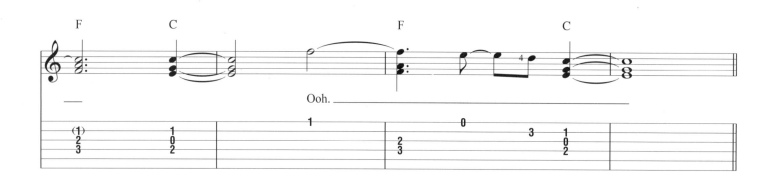

Verse

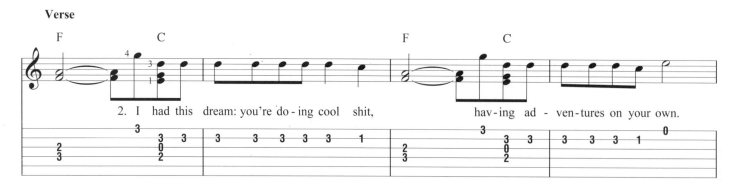

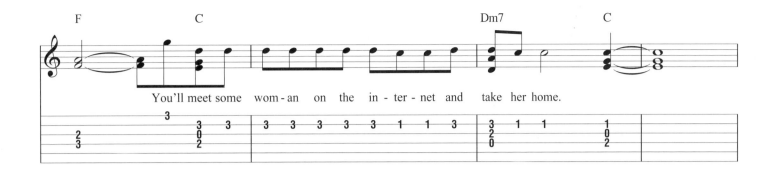

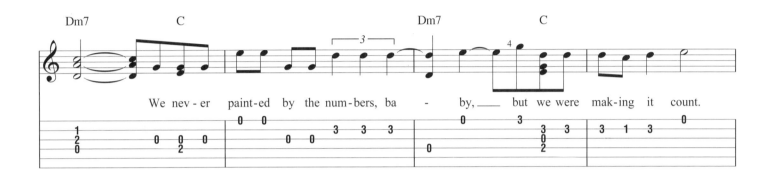

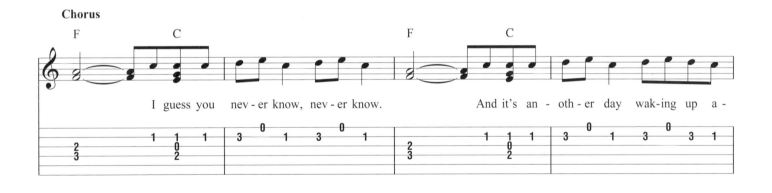

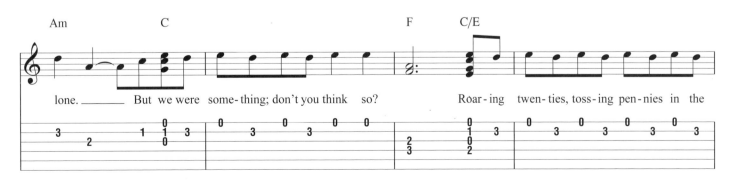

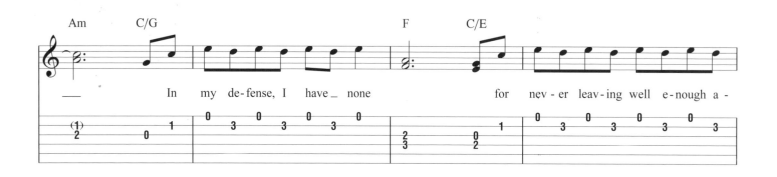

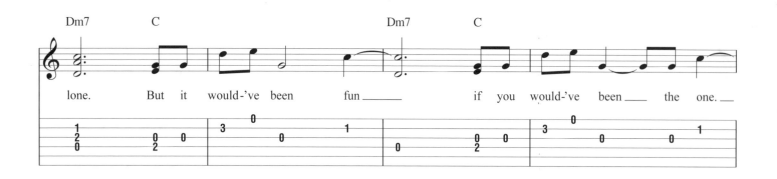

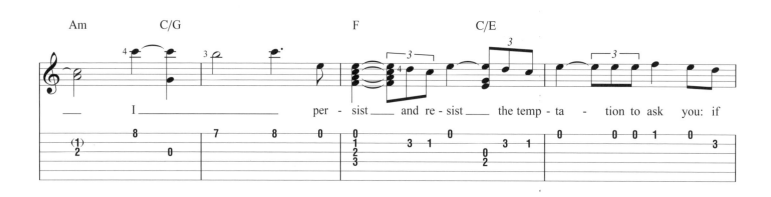

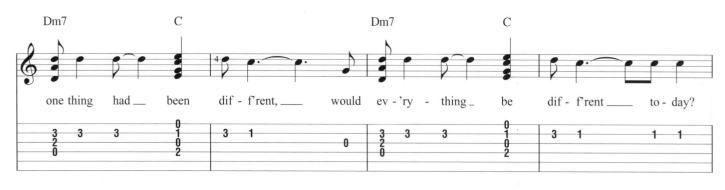

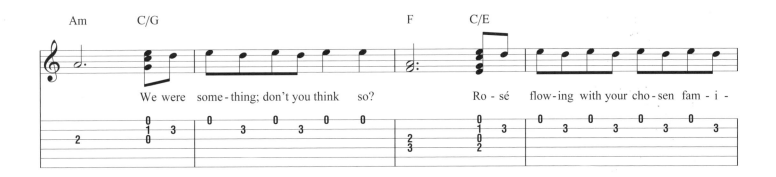

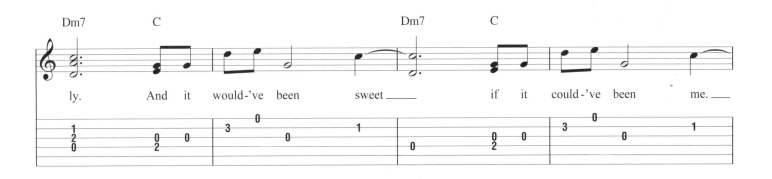

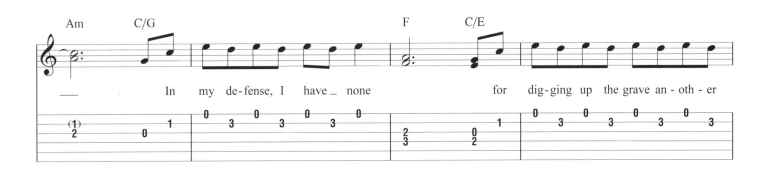

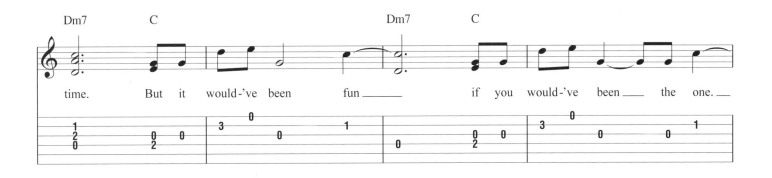

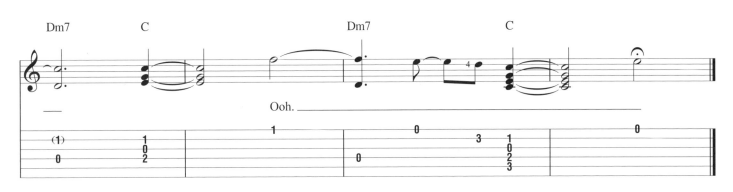

Our Song

Words and Music by Taylor Swift

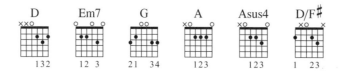

Strum Pattern: 2, 5
Pick Pattern: 1, 3

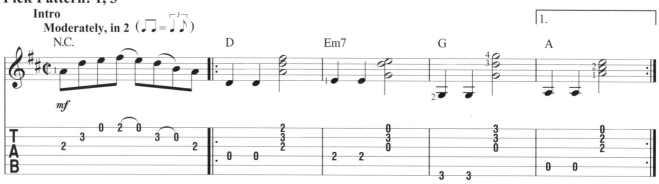

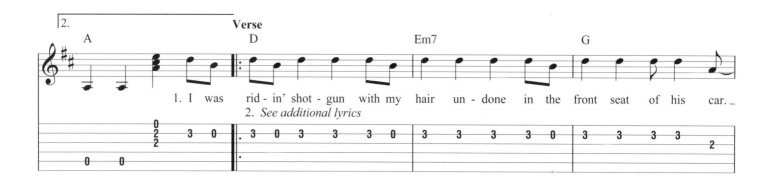

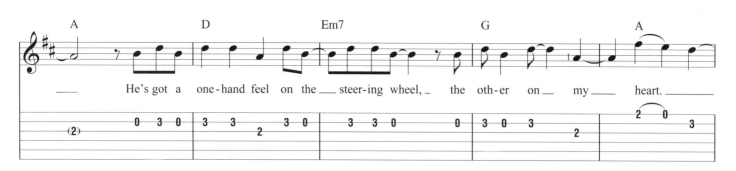

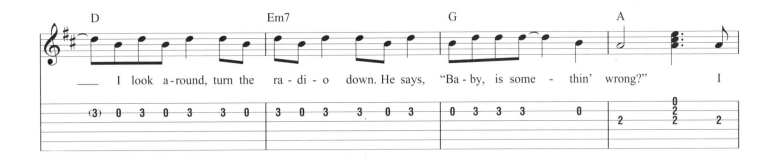

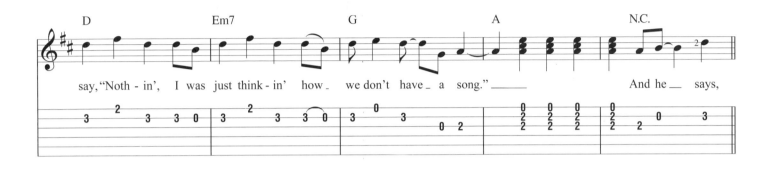

Chorus

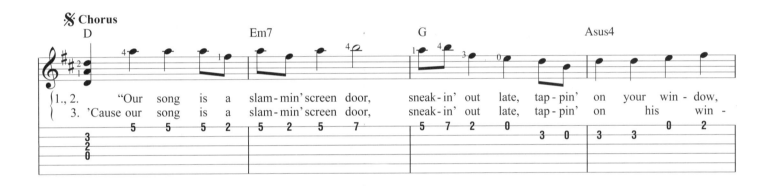

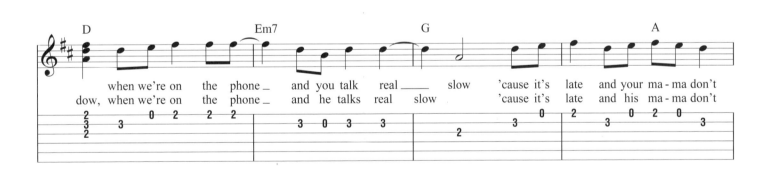

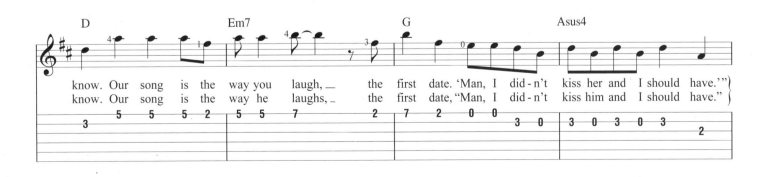

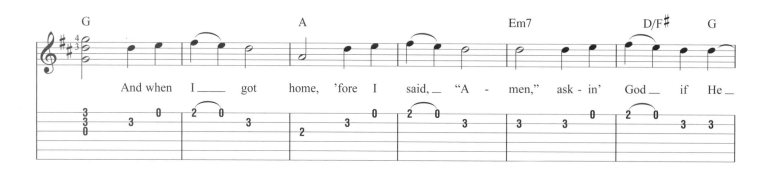

And when I ___ got home, 'fore I said, ___ "A - men," ask - in' God ___ if He ___

To Coda

Interlude

1.

___ could play it a - gain. ___

2.

Da, da, da, da. ___

I've

Bridge

heard ev - 'ry al - bum, lis - tened to the ra - di - o, wait - ed for some - thin' to come

D.S. al Coda

Coda

a - long that was as good as our ___ song. ___

*Let chord ring.

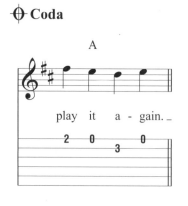

play it a - gain.

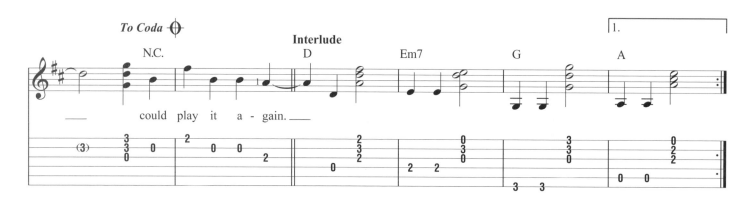
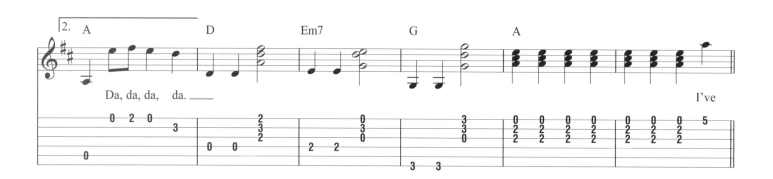

64

Interlude

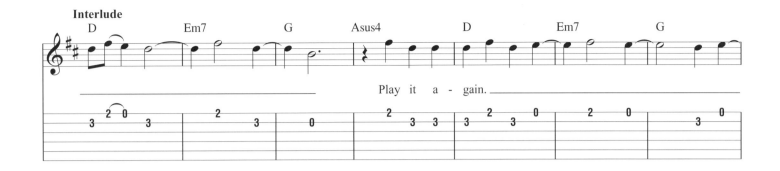

Play it a - gain.

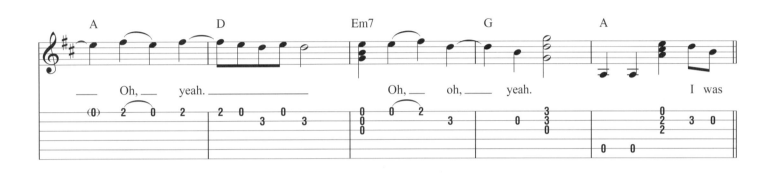

Oh, yeah. Oh, oh, yeah. I was

Outro

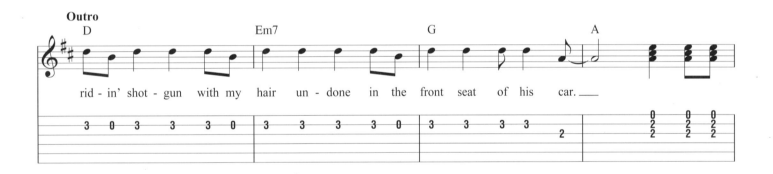

rid - in' shot - gun with my hair un - done in the front seat of his car.

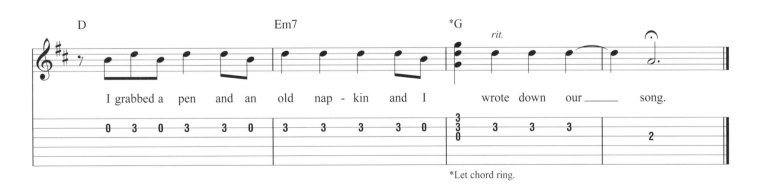

I grabbed a pen and an old nap - kin and I wrote down our song.

*Let chord ring.

Additional Lyrics

2. I was walkin' up the front porch steps after ev'rything that day
   Had gone all wrong, had been trampled on and lost and thrown away.
   Got to the hallway, well on my way to my lovin' bed.
   I almost didn't notice all the roses and the note that said...

Picture to Burn

Words and Music by Taylor Swift and Liz Rose

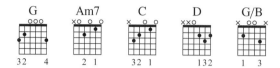

*Strum Pattern: 3, 4
*Pick Pattern: 4, 6

Intro
Moderately

*Use Pattern 10 for 2/4 measures.

Verse

1. State the ob - vi - ous,__ I did - n't get__ my per - fect fan - ta - sy.__
2. *See additional lyrics*

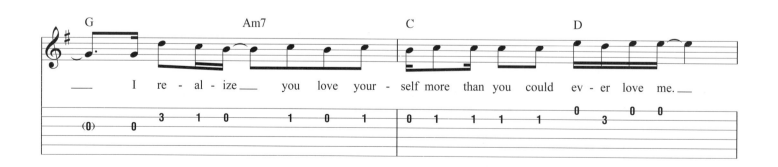

__ I re - al - ize__ you love your - self more than you could ev - er love me.__

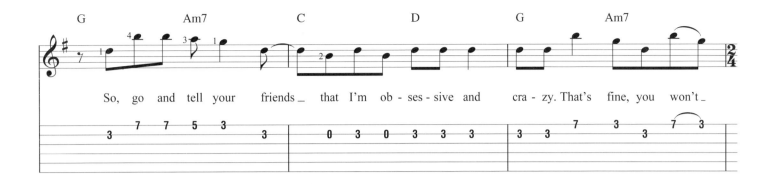

So, go and tell your friends _ that I'm ob - ses - sive and cra - zy. That's fine, you won't _

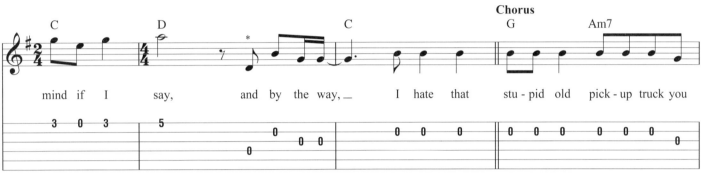

mind if I say, and by the way, _ I hate that stu - pid old pick - up truck you

*Sung one octave higher throughout chorus.

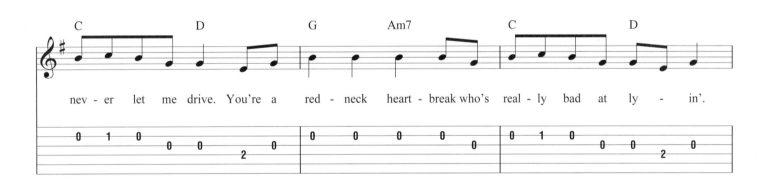

nev - er let me drive. You're a red - neck heart - break who's real - ly bad at ly - in'.

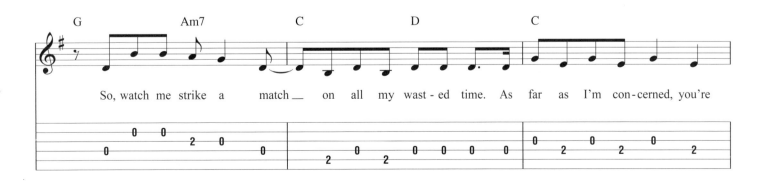

So, watch me strike a match _ on all my wast - ed time. As far as I'm con - cerned, you're

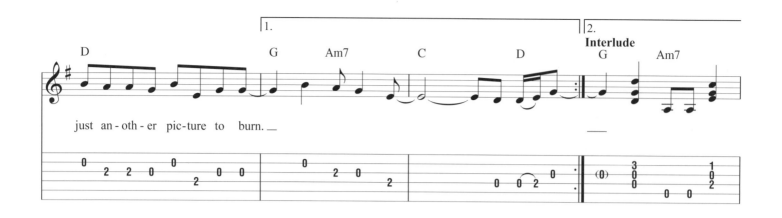

just an-oth-er pic-ture to burn. _

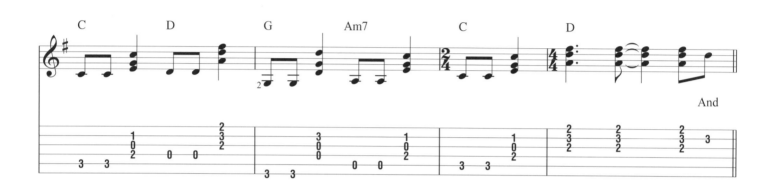

And

Bridge

if you're miss-in' me, you bet-ter keep it to your-self, 'cause com-in' back a-round here would be

Chorus

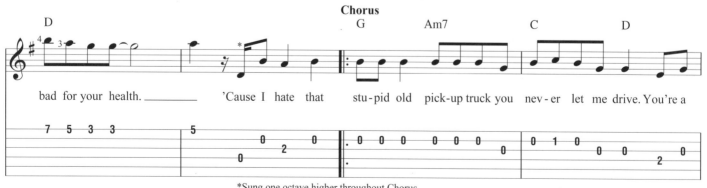

bad for your health. _____ 'Cause I hate that stu-pid old pick-up truck you nev-er let me drive. You're a

*Sung one octave higher throughout Chorus.

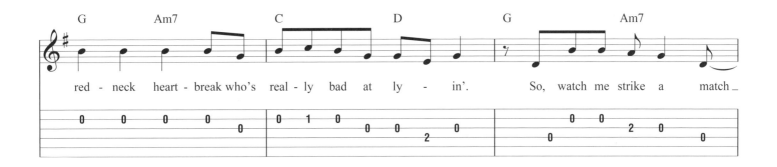

red - neck heart - break who's real - ly bad at ly - in'. So, watch me strike a match

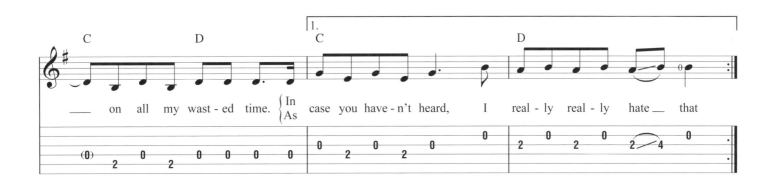

__ on all my wast - ed time. {In case you have - n't heard, I real - ly real - ly hate __ that
{As

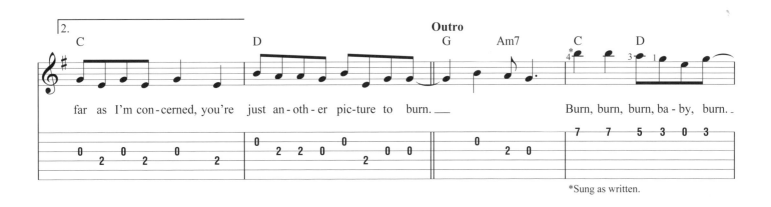

far as I'm con - cerned, you're just an - oth - er pic - ture to burn. __ Burn, burn, burn, ba - by, burn. __

*Sung as written.

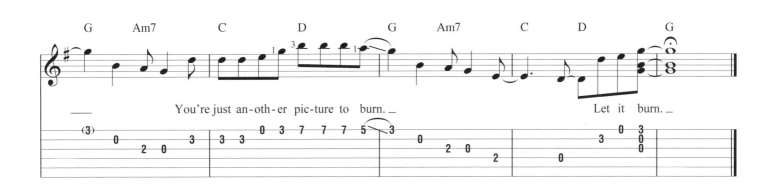

__ You're just an - oth - er pic - ture to burn. __ Let it burn. __

Additional Lyrics

2. There's no time for tears,
   I'm just sittin' here plannin' my revenge.
   There's nothin' stoppin' me,
   I'm going out with all of your best friends.
   And if you come around sayin' "sorry" to me,
   My daddy's gonna show you how sorry you'll be.
   'Cause I hate that...

...Ready for It?

Words and Music by Taylor Swift, Max Martin, Shellback and Ali Payami

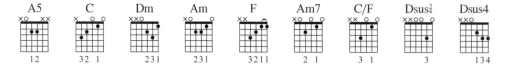

*Capo VII

Strum Pattern: 3
Pick Pattern: 3

Intro
Moderately slow, in 2

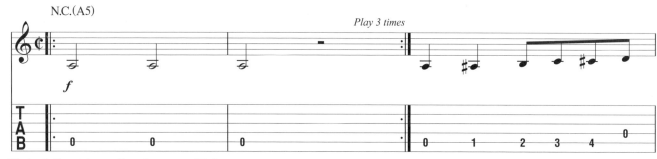

*Optional: To match recording, place capo at 7th fret.

Verse

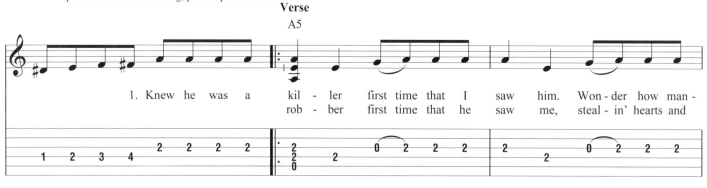

1. Knew he was a kil - ler first time that I saw him. Won - der how man -
   rob - ber first time that he saw me, steal - in' hearts and

y girls he had loved and left haunt - ed. But if he's a ghost, then I can be a
run - nin' off and nev - er say - in' sor - ry. But if I'm a thief, then he can join the

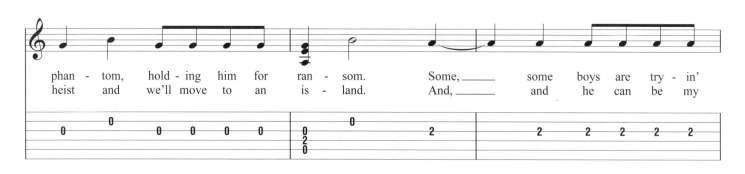

phan - tom, hold - ing him for ran - som. Some, _____ some boys are try - in'
heist and we'll move to an is - land. And, _____ and he can be my

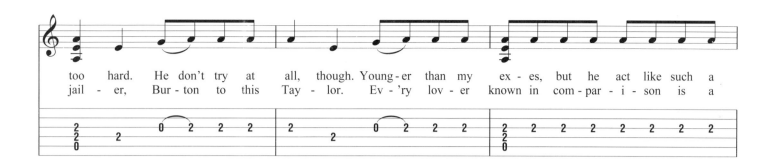

too hard. He don't try at all, though. Young-er than my ex-es, but he act like such a
jail - er, Bur - ton to this Tay - lor. Ev - 'ry lov - er known in com-par - i - son is a

man, so I see noth - ing bet - ter. I keep him for - ev - er like a ven -
fail - ure. I for - get their names now. I'm so ver - y tame now. Nev - er be the

Pre-Chorus

A5

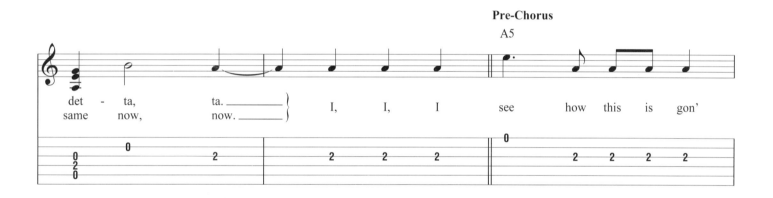

det - ta, ta. _____ } I, I, I see how this is gon'
same now, now. _____ }

go. Touch me and you'll nev - er be a - lone. I, is - land

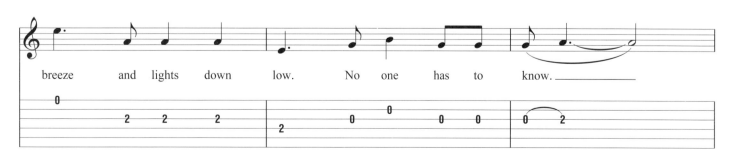

breeze and lights down low. No one has to know. _____

%% **Chorus**

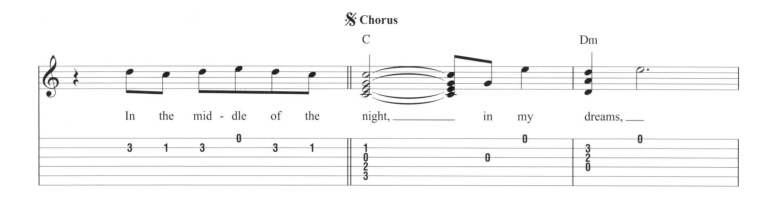

In the mid-dle of the night, _____ in my dreams, _____

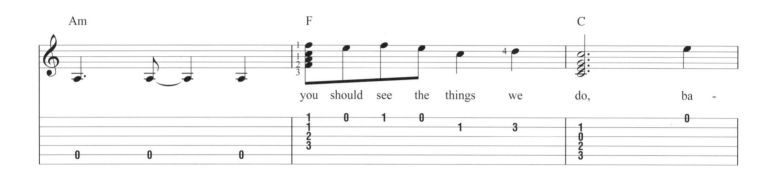

you should see the things we do, ba -

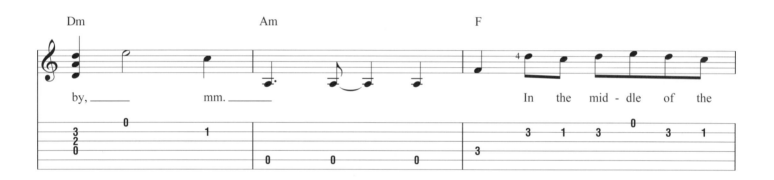

by, _____ mm. _____ In the mid-dle of the

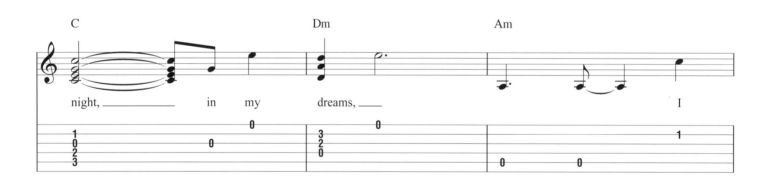

night, _____ in my dreams, _____ I

3rd time, To Coda

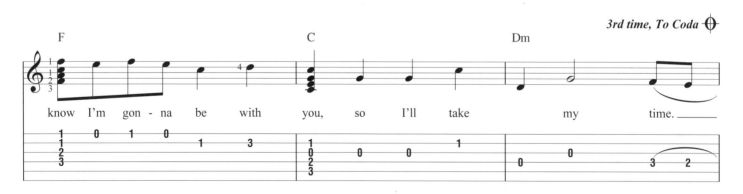

know I'm gon-na be with you, so I'll take my time. _____

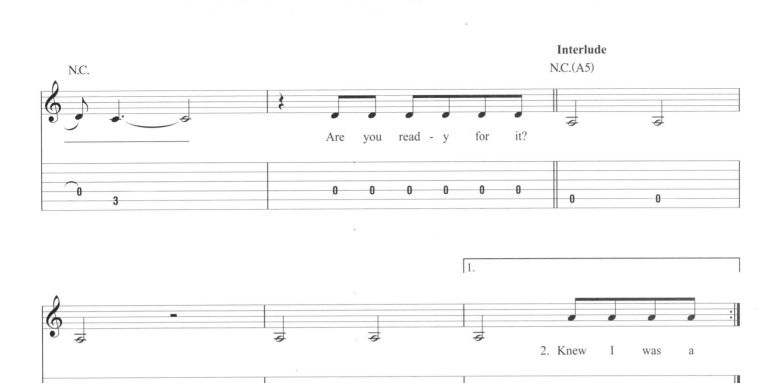

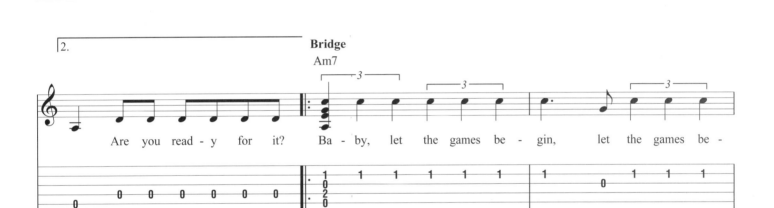

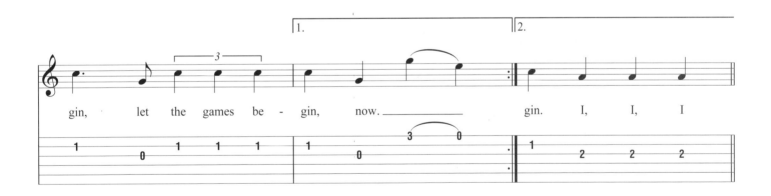

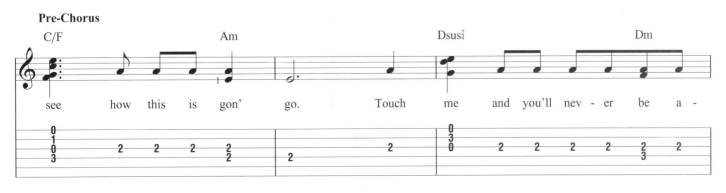

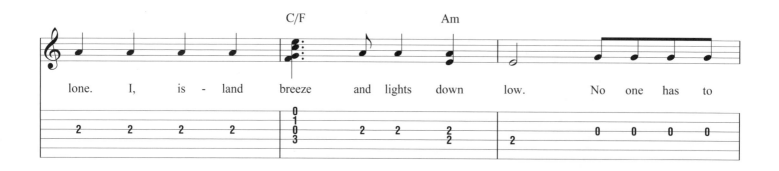

lone. I, is - land breeze and lights down low. No one has to

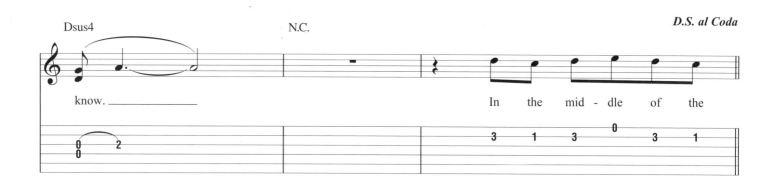

D.S. al Coda

know. _____ In the mid - dle of the

Coda

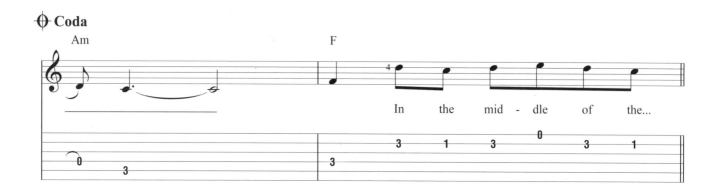

_____ In the mid - dle of the...

Outro

Ba - by, let the games be - gin, let the games be - gin, let the games be -

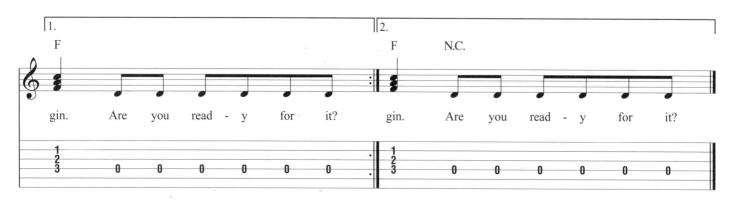

1.   2.

gin. Are you read - y for it?   gin. Are you read - y for it?

Safe & Sound

from THE HUNGER GAMES

Words and Music by Taylor Swift, T-Bone Burnett, John Paul White and Joy Williams

*Optional: To match recording, place capo at 7th fret.

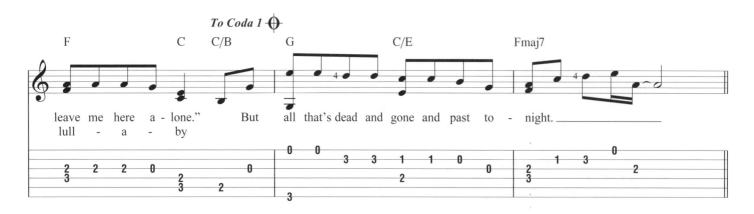

leave me here a - lone." But all that's dead and gone and past to - night. _____
lull - a - by

Chorus

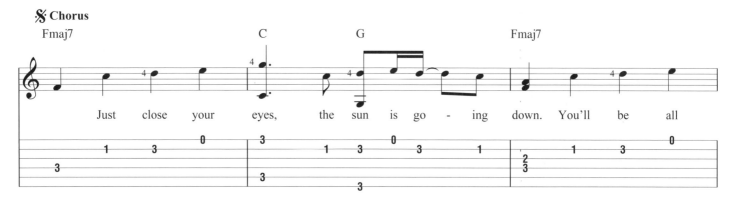

Just close your eyes, the sun is go - ing down. You'll be all

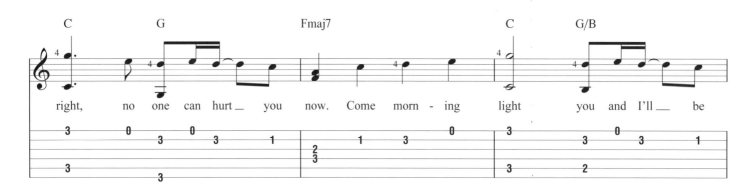

right, no one can hurt ___ you now. Come morn - ing light you and I'll ___ be

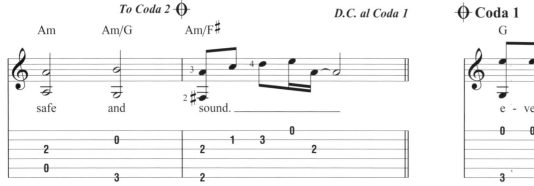

safe and sound. _____

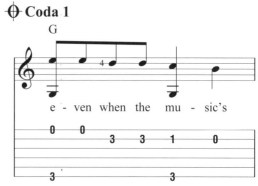

e - ven when the mu - sic's

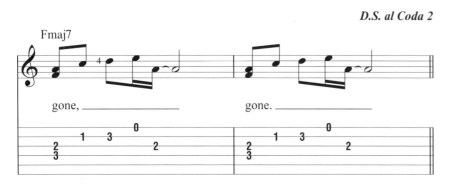

gone, _____ gone. _____

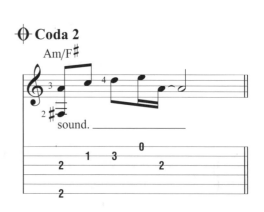

sound. _____

76

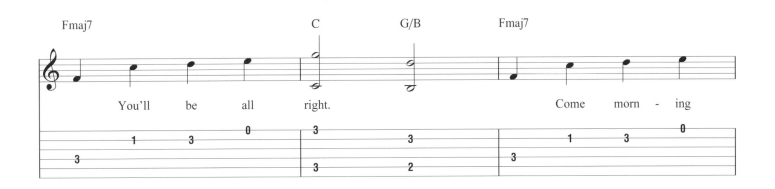

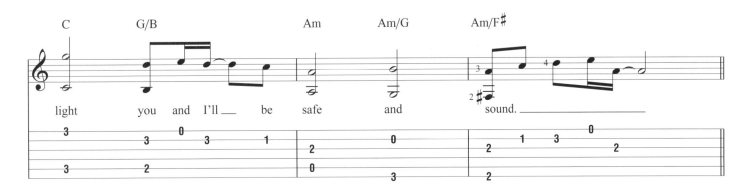

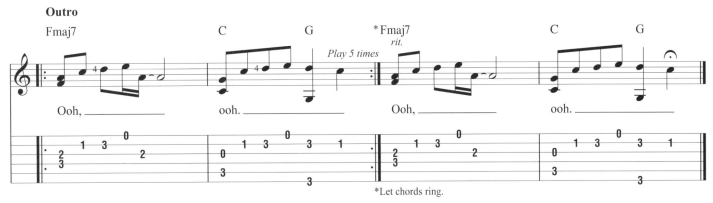

Shake It Off

Words and Music by Taylor Swift, Max Martin and Shellback

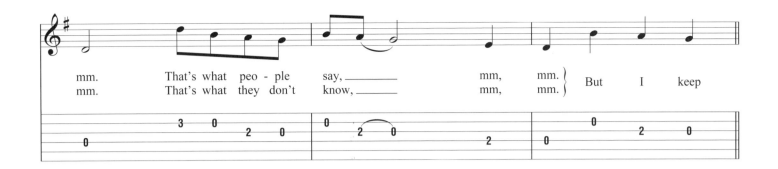

mm. That's what peo - ple say, _____ mm, mm.
mm. That's what they don't know, _____ mm, mm. } But I keep

Pre-Chorus

cruis - ing; can't stop, won't stop { mov - ing. }{ groov - ing. } It's like I got this

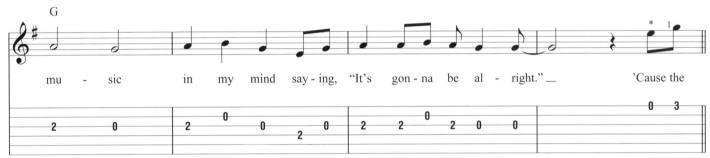

mu - sic in my mind say - ing, "It's gon - na be al - right." _ 'Cause the

*Sung as written.

𝄋 **Chorus**

play - ers gon - na play, play, play, play, play, and the hat - ers gon - na hate, hate,

hate, hate, hate. Ba - by, I'm just gon - na shake, shake, shake, shake, shake. _ I

79

Am

shake it off,___ I shake it   off.   Heart - break-ers gon-na break, break,   break, break, break, and the

C   G

fak - ers gon - na fake, fake,   fake, fake, fake.   Ba - by,   I'm just gon - na shake, shake,

|1. |2.

To Coda ⊕

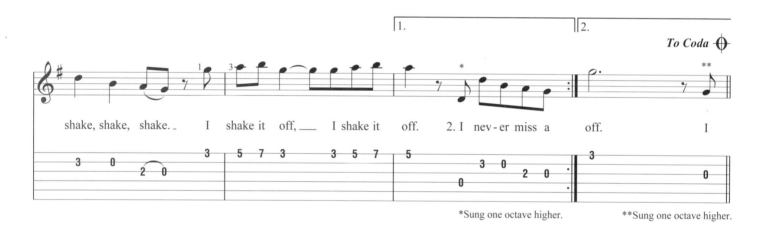

shake, shake, shake._   I shake it off,___ I shake it   off.   2. I nev-er miss a   off.   I

*Sung one octave higher.   **Sung one octave higher.

Bridge

Am   C

shake it off,___ I shake it   off.   I,___   I,   I shake it off,___   I shake it   off.   I,___   I,   I

G

shake it off,___ I shake it   off.   I,___   I,   I shake it off,___   I shake it   off.

Breakdown

N.C.

Spoken: "Hey, hey, hey!   *Just think: while you've been gettin' down and out about the liars and the dirty,*

dirty cheats of the world, you   could've been gettin' down to   this!   sick!   beat!"

Rap: My   ex   man brought his   new   girl-friend. She's like, "Oh   my   God!" But   I'm just gon-na shake. And to the

fel - la   o - ver there with the   hell - a   good   hair, won't you   come on   o - ver, ba - by? We can

D.S. al Coda
(take 2nd ending)

shake,   shake,   shake.   Yeah, _____   oh. _____   'Cause the

*Sung one octave higher.   **Sung as written.

⊕ Coda

Outro

Am   C

⎰ 1. shake ⎱ it off, ____ I shake it   off. I, ____ I,   I shake it   off, ____ I shake it   off. I, ____ I,   I
⎱ 2., 3. Shake ⎰

|1., 2.| |3.|

G

shake it   off, ____ I shake it   off. I, ____ I,   I shake it   off, ____ I shake it   off.   off.

Should've Said No

Words and Music by Taylor Swift

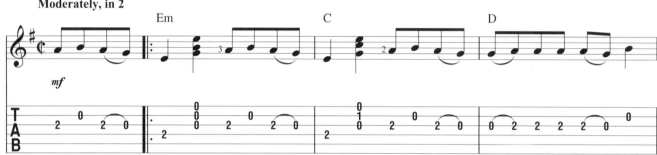

Strum Pattern: 5
Pick Pattern: 1

Intro
Moderately, in 2

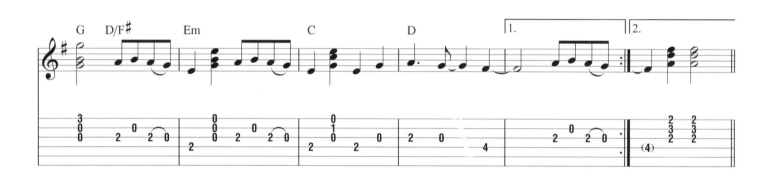

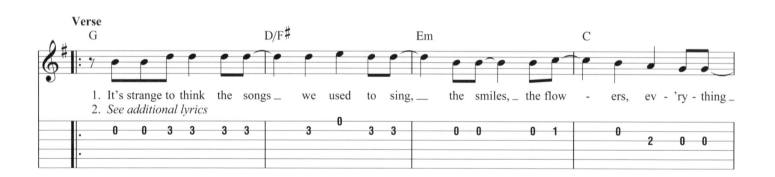

Verse

1. It's strange to think the songs _ we used to sing, _ the smiles, _ the flow - ers, ev - 'ry - thing _
2. See additional lyrics

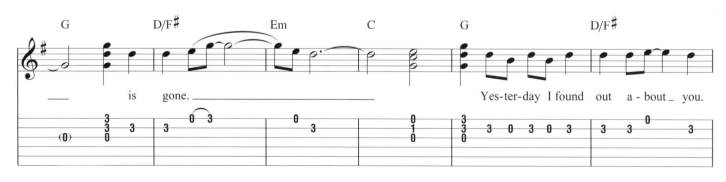

_ is gone. _____ Yes-ter-day I found out a-bout _ you.

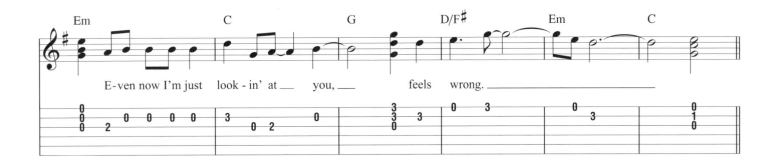

E-ven now I'm just look-in' at ___ you, ___ feels wrong. _____

Pre-Chorus

You say ___ that you'd take it all back giv-en one chance.)
You say ___ that the past is the past. You need one chance.)
It was a mo-ment of

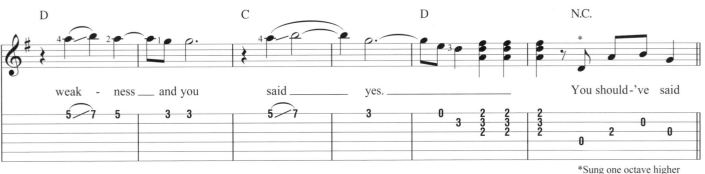

weak - ness ___ and you said _____ yes. _____ You should-'ve said

*Sung one octave higher
throughout Chorus.

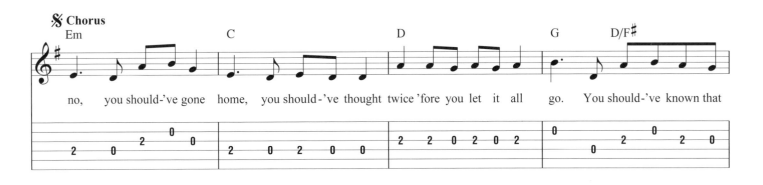

𝄋 Chorus

no, you should-'ve gone home, you should-'ve thought twice 'fore you let it all go. You should-'ve known that

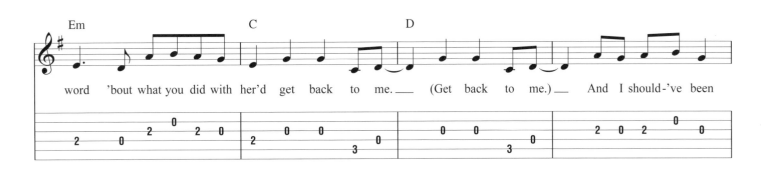

word 'bout what you did with her'd get back to me. ___ (Get back to me.) ___ And I should-'ve been

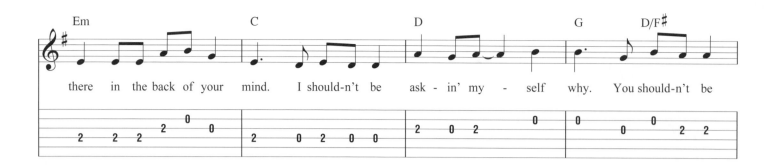

there   in the back of your   mind.   I should-n't be   ask - in' my - self   why.   You should-n't be

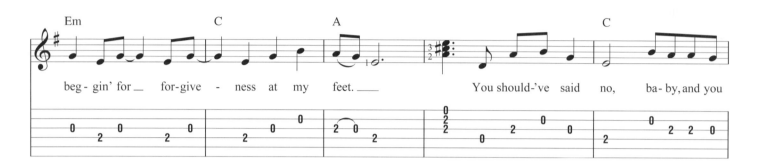

beg- gin' for __ for-give - ness at   my   feet. ___   You should-'ve said   no,   ba- by, and you

To Coda ✦ |1.
Interlude

might still   have   me. _____

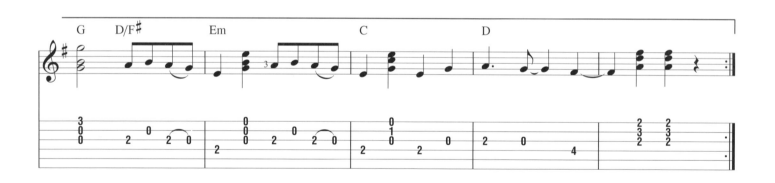

|2.
Guitar Solo

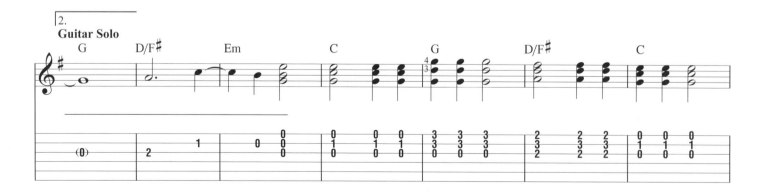

Bridge

I can't re - sist. ___ Be-fore you go, tell me this: ___

*Sung one octave higher throughout Bridge.

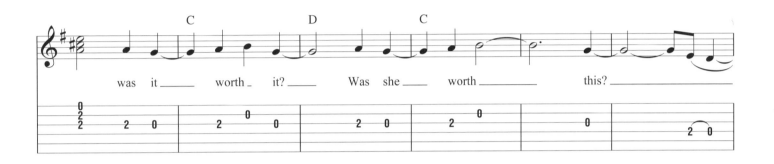

was it ___ worth _ it? ___ Was she ___ worth ___ this? ___

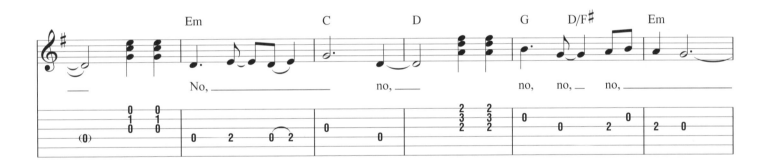

___ No, ___ no, ___ no, no, ___ no,

Coda

D.S. al Coda

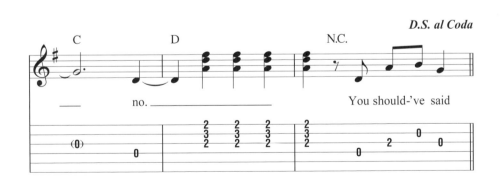

___ no. ___ You should-'ve said

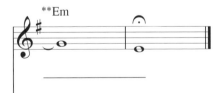

**Em

**Let chord ring.

Additional Lyrics

2. You can see that I've been cryin',
Baby, you know all the right things to say.
But do you honestly expect me to believe
We could ever be the same?

Teardrops on My Guitar

Words and Music by Taylor Swift and Liz Rose

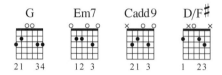

*Capo III

Strum Pattern: 3, 6
Pick Pattern: 2, 5

Intro
Moderately

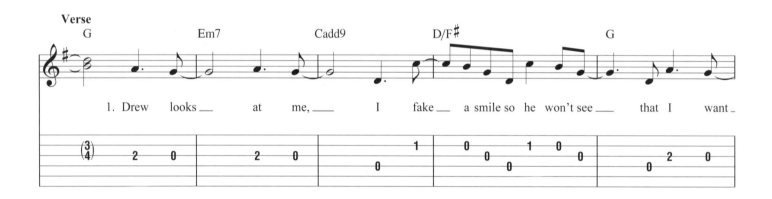

*Optional: To match recording, place capo at 3rd fret.

Verse

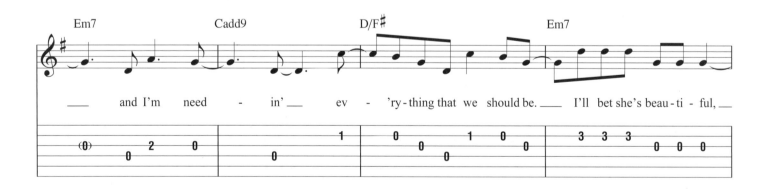

1. Drew looks ___ at me, ___ I fake ___ a smile so he won't see ___ that I want ___ and I'm need - in' ___ ev - 'ry-thing that we should be. ___ I'll bet she's beau - ti - ful,

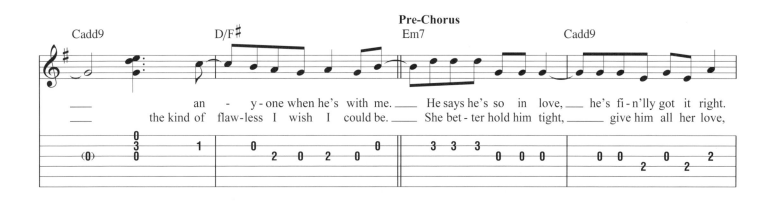

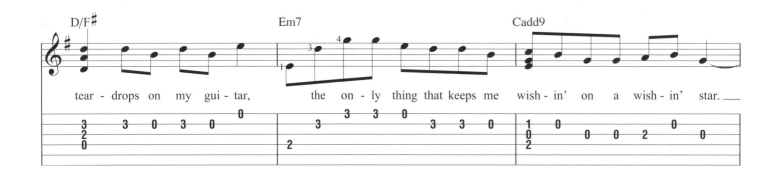

tear - drops on my gui - tar, the on - ly thing that keeps me wish - in' on a wish - in' star. ___

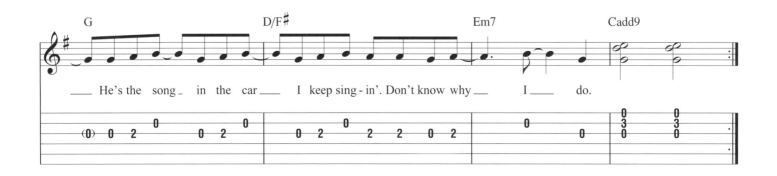

___ He's the song ___ in the car ___ I keep sing - in'. Don't know why ___ I ___ do.

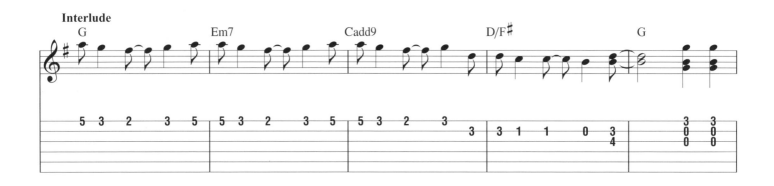

Interlude

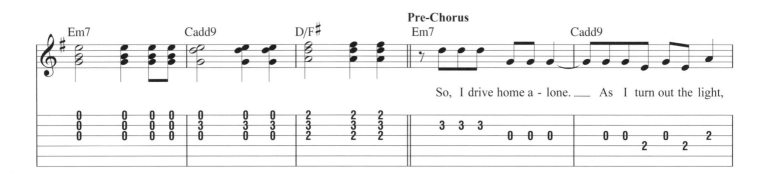

Pre-Chorus

So, I drive home a - lone. ___ As I turn out the light,

Chorus

I'll put his pic - ture down and may - be get some sleep to - night. 'Cause he's the rea - son for the

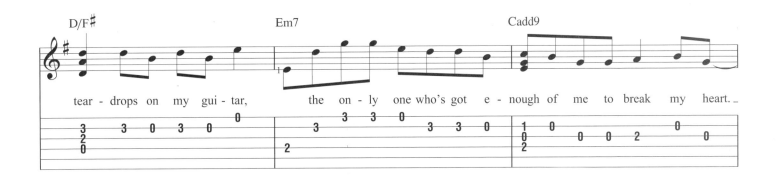

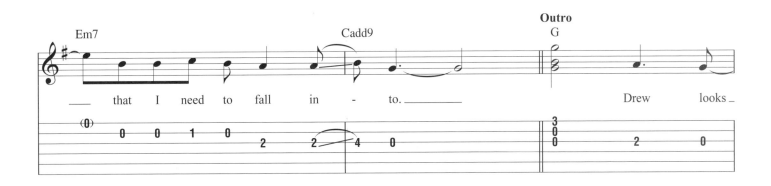

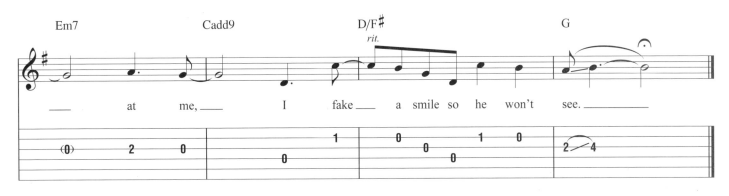

22

Words and Music by Taylor Swift, Max Martin and Shellback

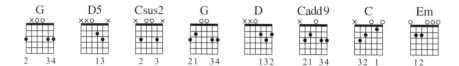

Strum Pattern: 5
Pick Pattern: 5

Intro
Moderately, in 2

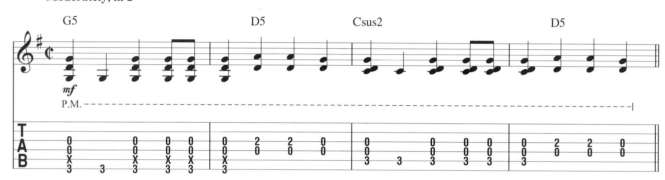

Verse

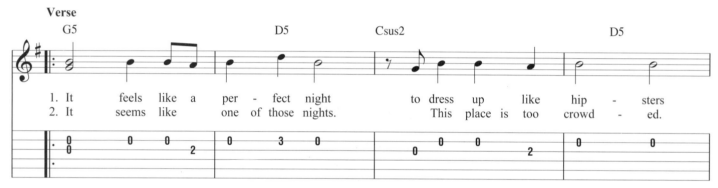

1. It feels like a per-fect night to dress up like hip-sters
2. It seems like one of those nights. This place is too crowd-ed.

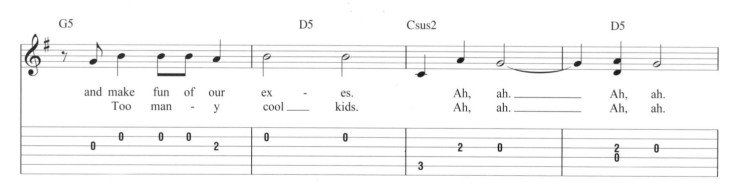

and make fun of our ex - es. Ah, ah. _____ Ah, ah.
Too man - y cool _____ kids. Ah, ah. _____ Ah, ah.

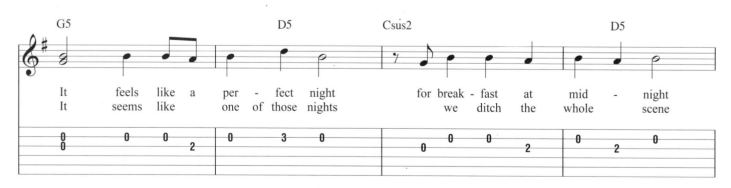

It feels like a per - fect night for break - fast at mid - night
It seems like one of those nights we ditch the whole scene

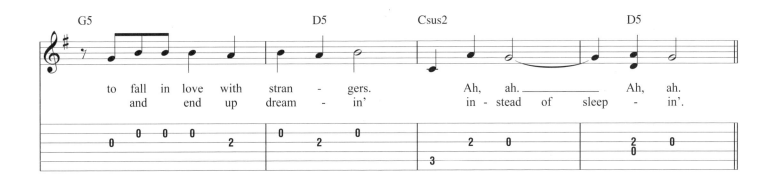

Pre-Chorus

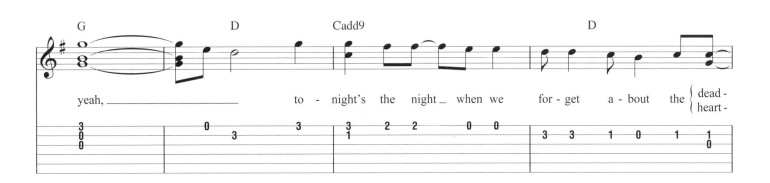

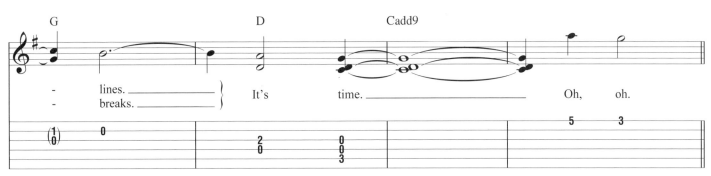

*Sung one octave higher throughout Chorus and Bridge.

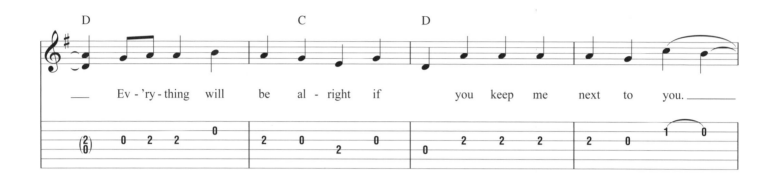

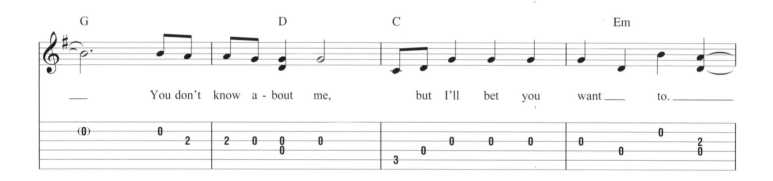

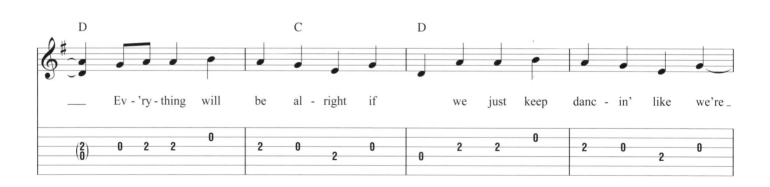

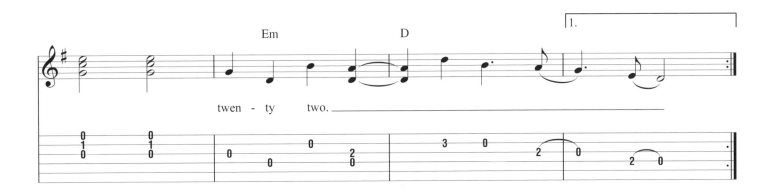

twen - ty two. _____

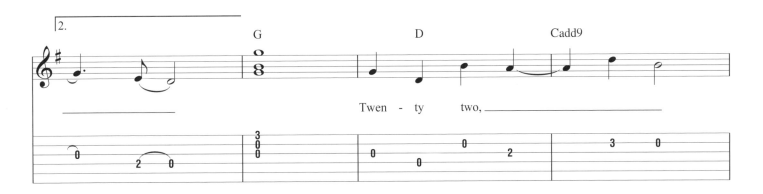

Twen - ty two, _____

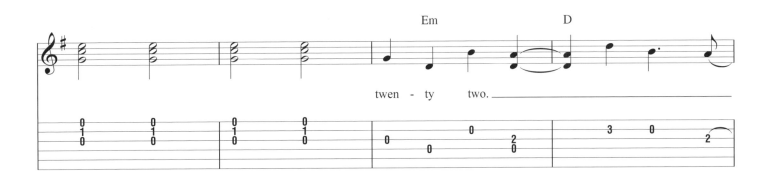

twen - ty two. _____

Bridge

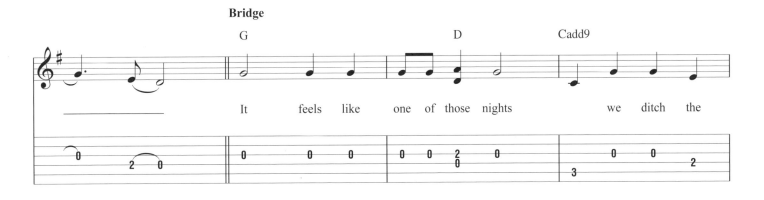

It feels like one of those nights we ditch the

whole scene. It feels like one of those nights

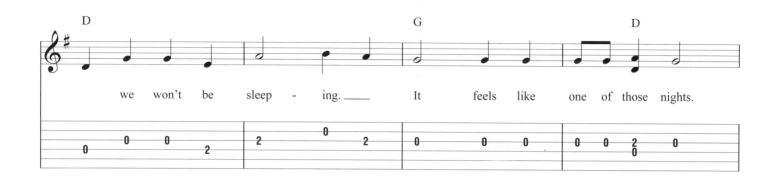

we won't be sleep - ing. _____ It feels like one of those nights.

To Coda ⊕

You look like bad news. I got - ta have _____ you,

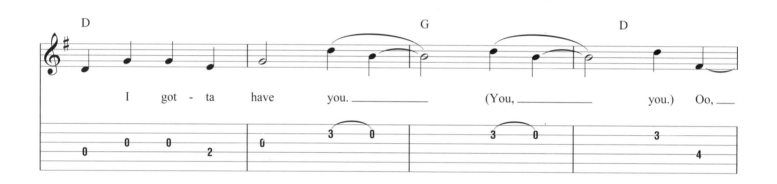

I got - ta have you. _____ (You, _____ you.) Oo, _____

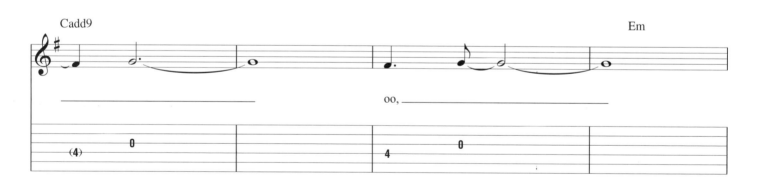

oo, _____

D.S. al Coda
(take 2nd ending)

⊕ **Coda**

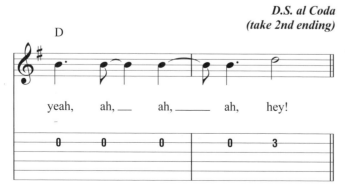

yeah, ah, _____ ah, _____ ah, hey!

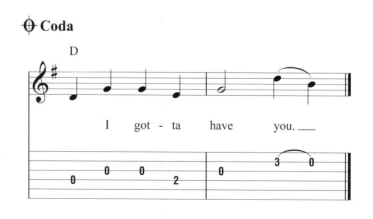

I got - ta have you. _____

We Are Never Ever Getting Back Together

Words and Music by Taylor Swift, Max Martin and Shellback

Strum Pattern: 5
Pick Pattern: 1

Intro
Moderately, in 2

*Knock on guitar body w/ right hand.

Verse

1. I re-mem-ber when we broke _ up the first time, say-ing,"This is it. I've had e-

nough." 'Cause like, we had-n't seen each oth-er in a month when you said you need-ed

space. **Spoken: What?*

Then you come a-round a-gain and say, "Ba-by, I
real-ly gon-na miss you pick-ing fights. And me,

**Lyrics in italics are spoken throughout.

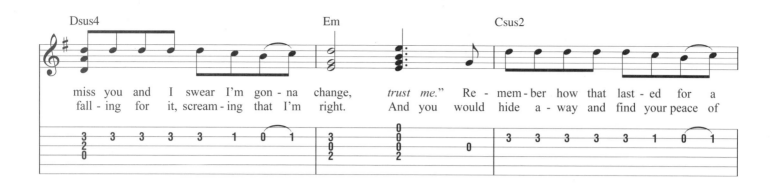

miss you and I swear I'm gon - na change, *trust me.*" Re - mem - ber how that last - ed for a
fall - ing for it, scream - ing that I'm right. And you would hide a - way and find your peace of

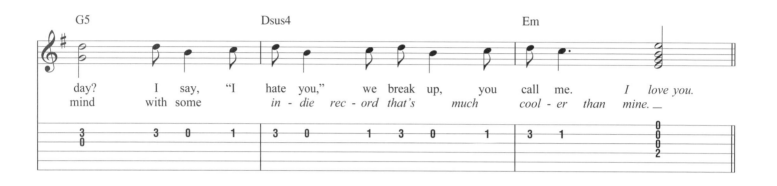

day? I say, "I hate you," we break up, you call me. I love you.
mind with some *in - die rec - ord that's much cool - er than mine.*

Pre-Chorus

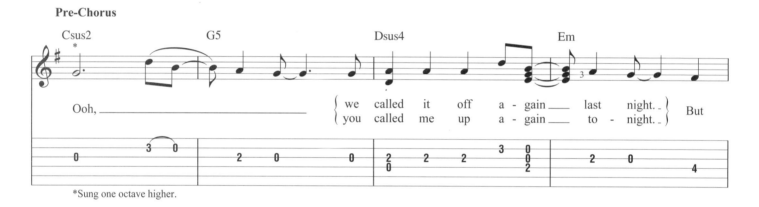

Ooh, _____
we called it off a - gain _____ last night. _
you called me up a - gain _____ to - night. } But

*Sung one octave higher.

ooh, _____ this time _____ I'm tell - ing you, I'm tell - ing you

Chorus

we are nev - er ev - er ev - er _____ get - ting back to - geth - er.

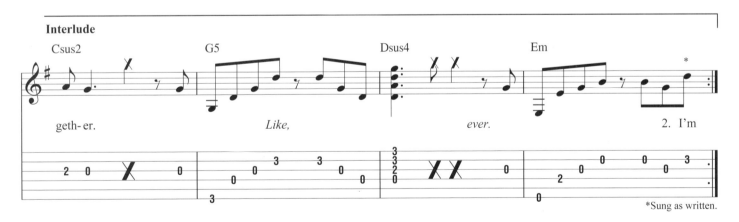

*Sung as written.

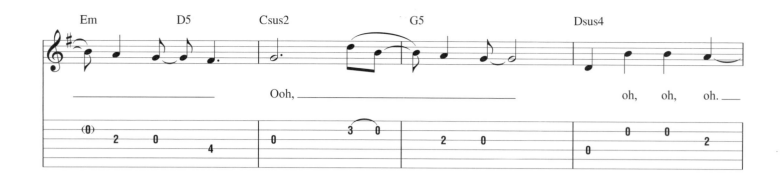

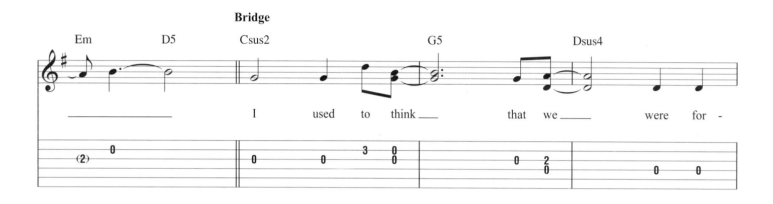

Bridge

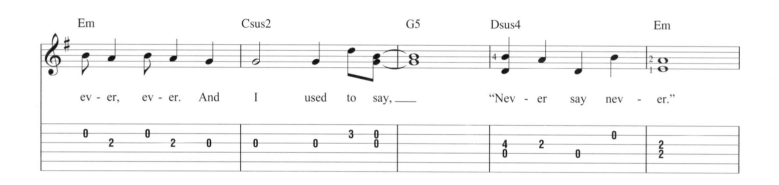

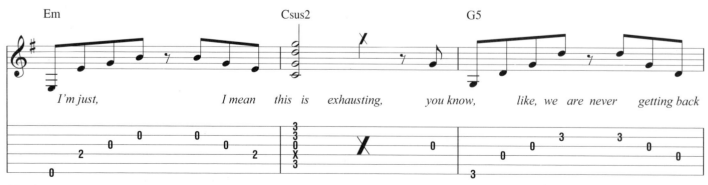

Chorus

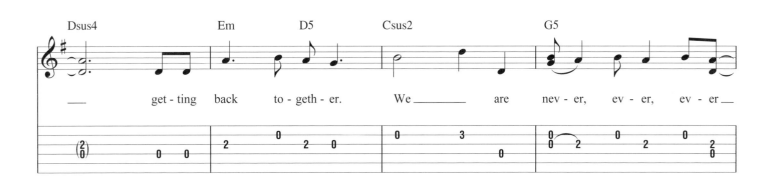

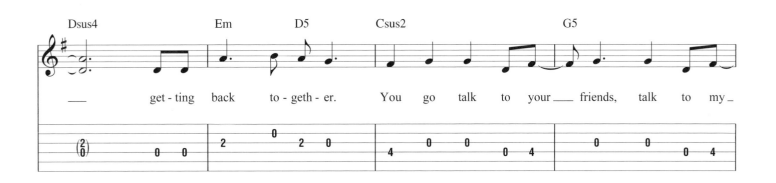

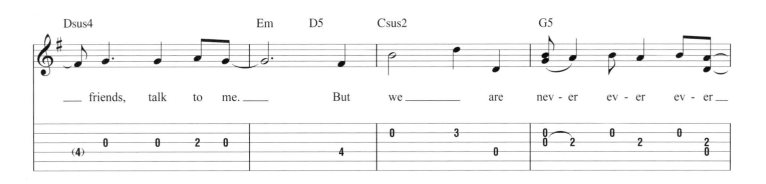

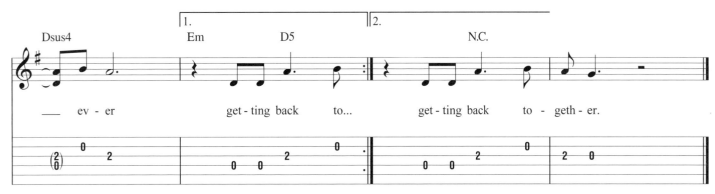

White Horse

Words and Music by Taylor Swift and Liz Rose

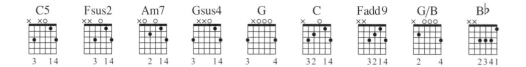

Strum Pattern: 3, 6
Pick Pattern: 2, 5

Intro
Moderately

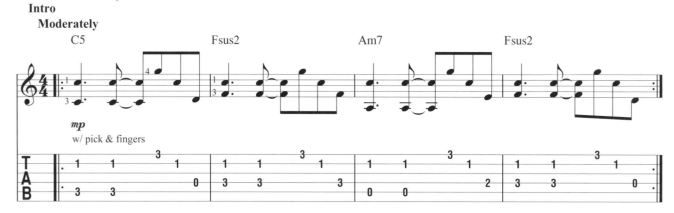

Verse

1. Say you're sor - ry, that face ___ of an an - gel comes out ___ just when you need it to

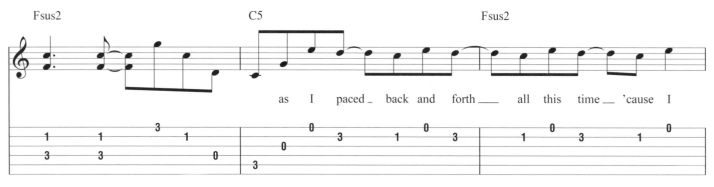

as I paced ___ back and forth ___ all this time ___ 'cause I

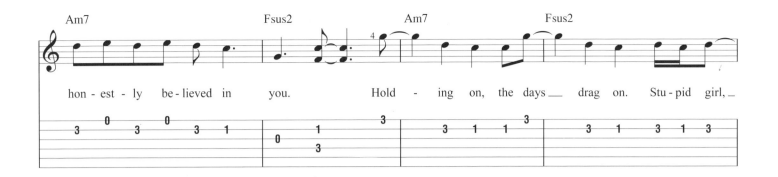

hon - est - ly be - lieved in you. Hold - ing on, the days ___ drag on. Stu - pid girl, ___

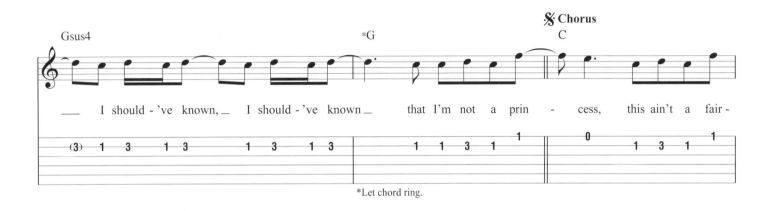

___ I should - 've known, ___ I should - 've known ___ that I'm not a prin - cess, this ain't a fair -

*Let chord ring.

y tale. I'm not the one ___ you'll sweep off her feet, lead her up the stair - well. This ain't

Hol - ly wood, this is a small ___ town. I was a dream - er be - fore you went and let

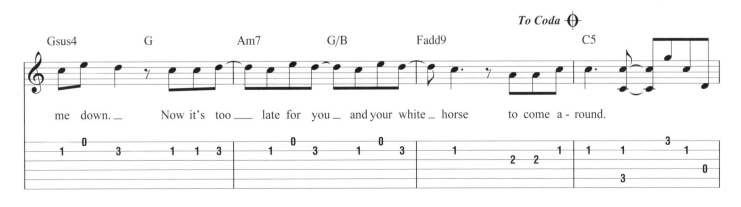

me down. ___ Now it's too ___ late for you ___ and your white ___ horse to come a - round.

Verse

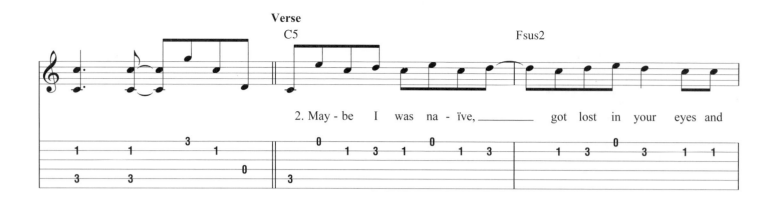

2. May - be I was na - ïve, _____ got lost in your eyes and

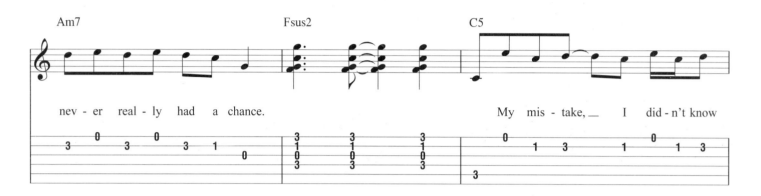

nev - er real - ly had a chance. My mis - take, _ I did - n't know

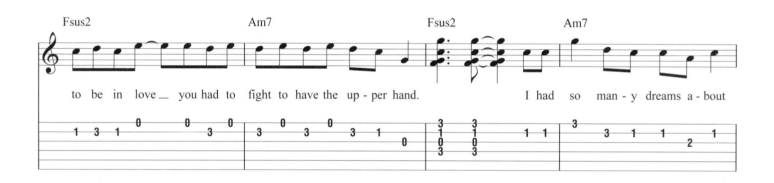

to be in love _ you had to fight to have the up - per hand. I had so man - y dreams a - bout

D.S. al Coda

you and me; _ hap - py end - ings, now _ I know _ that I'm not a prin -

*Let chord ring.

⊕ Coda

Guitar Solo

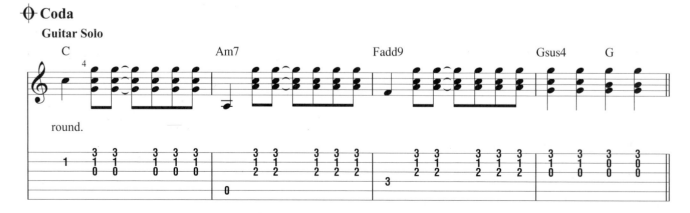

round.

102

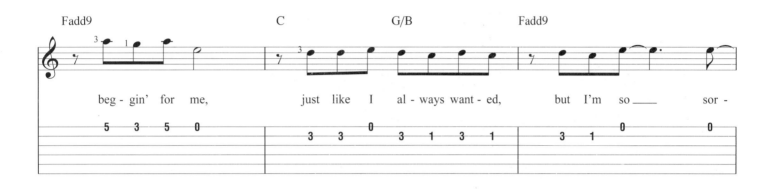

Chorus

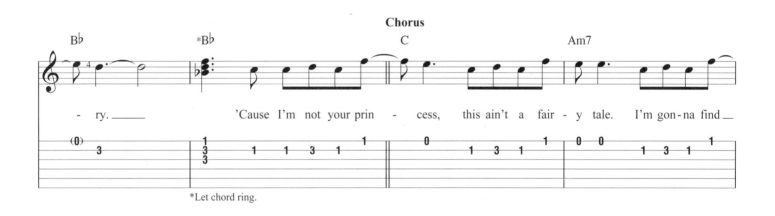

*Let chord ring.

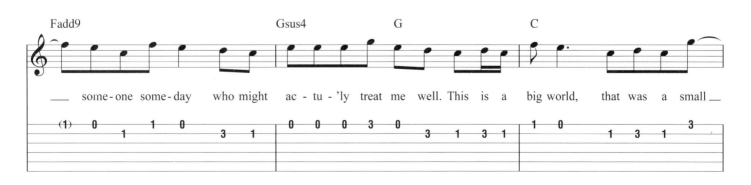

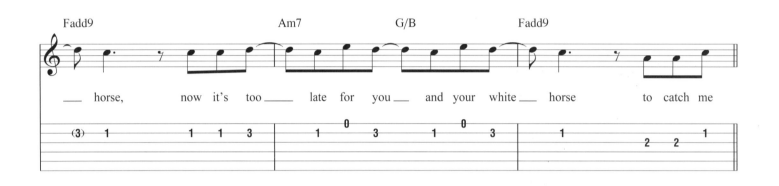

Outro

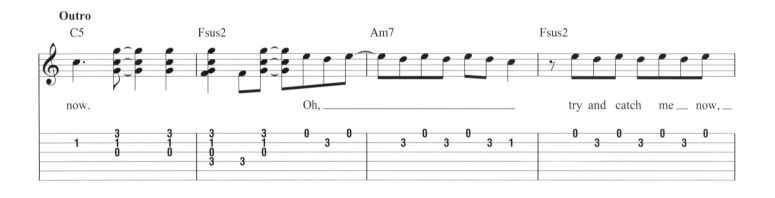

*Let chord ring.

You Belong with Me

Words and Music by Taylor Swift and Liz Rose

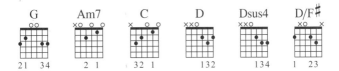

*Tune down 1/2 step:
(low to high) E♭-A♭-D♭-G♭-B♭-E♭

Strum Pattern: 1
Pick Pattern: 5

*Optional: To match recording, tune down 1/2 step.

I'm in the room, it's a typ-i-cal Tues-day night. __ I'm list'-nin' to the kind of mu-sic she does-n't like. __

___ And she'll nev-er know your sto-ry like I do. But

% Pre-Chorus

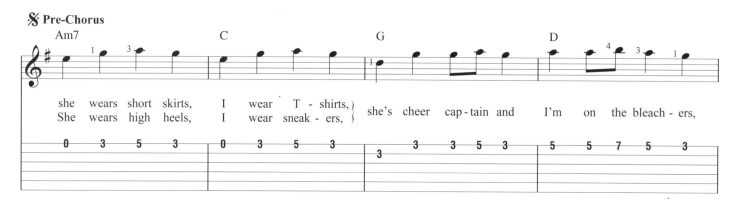

she wears short skirts, I wear T-shirts,
She wears high heels, I wear sneak-ers, } she's cheer cap-tain and I'm on the bleach-ers,

dream-in' 'bout the day when you wake up and find __ that what you're look-in' for __ has been here __

*Let chord ring.

Chorus

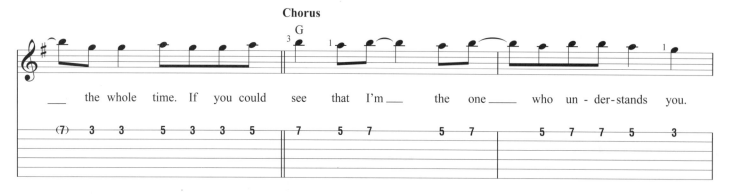

___ the whole time. If you could see that I'm __ the one __ who un-der-stands you.

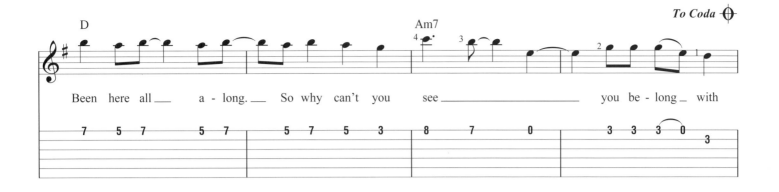

*Let chord ring.

Verse

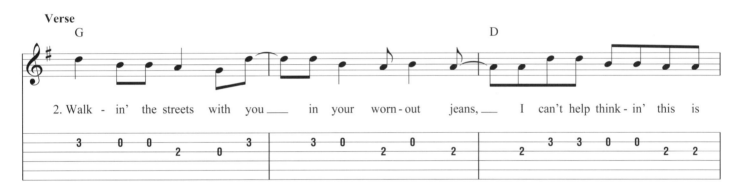

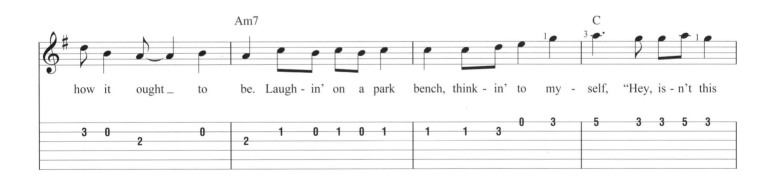

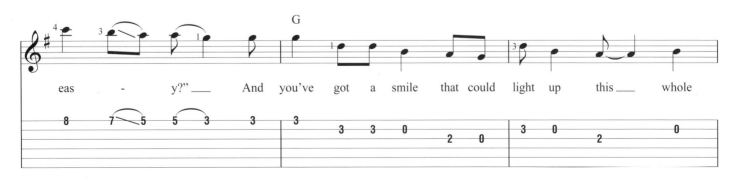

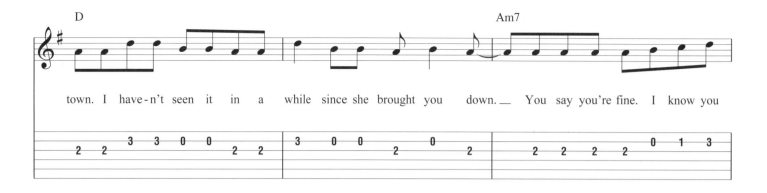

town. I have-n't seen it in a while since she brought you down.__ You say you're fine. I know you

D.S. al Coda

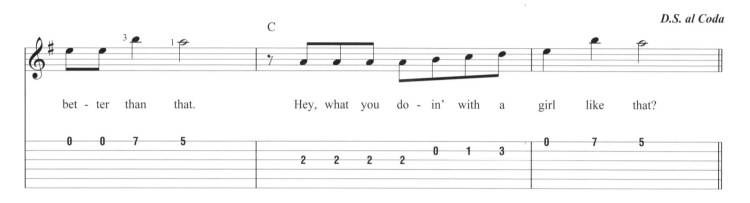

bet - ter than that. Hey, what you do - in' with a girl like that?

Coda

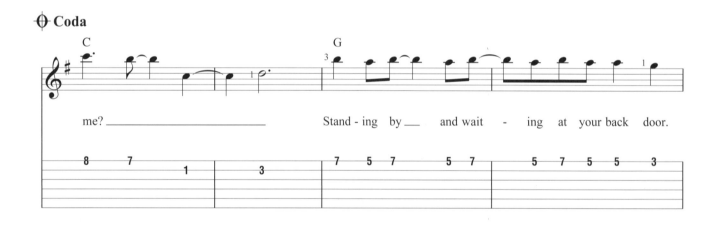

me? _____ Stand - ing by __ and wait - ing at your back door.

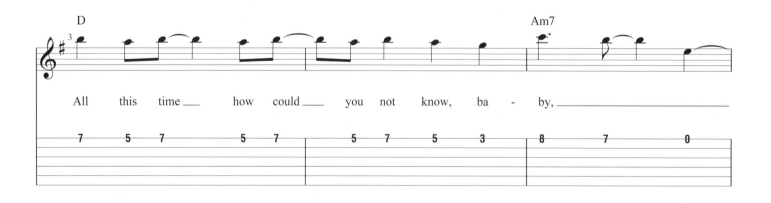

All this time __ how could __ you not know, ba - by, _____

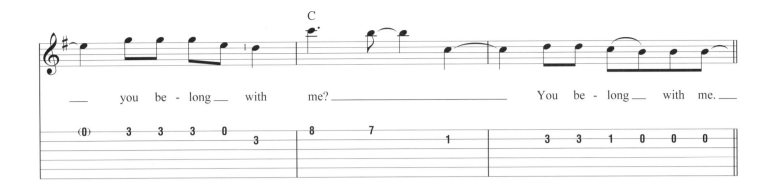

you be - long ___ with me? _____ You be - long ___ with me. ___

Interlude

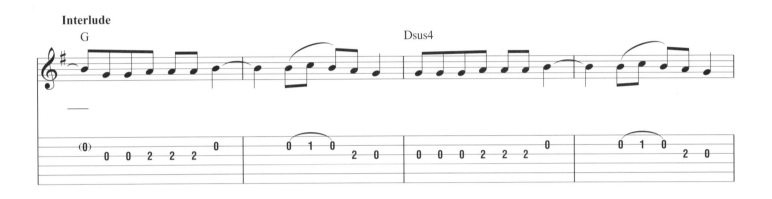

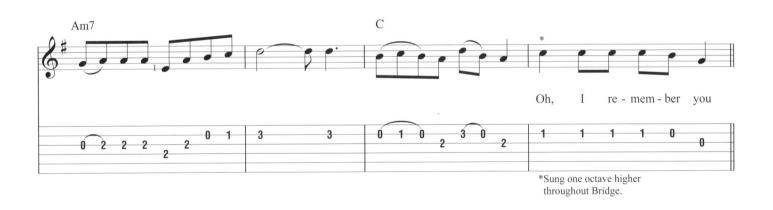

Oh, I re - mem - ber you

*Sung one octave higher
throughout Bridge.

Bridge

driv - in' to my house in the mid - dle of the night. I'm the one who makes you laugh when you

know you're 'bout to cry. I know your fav-'rite songs and you tell me 'bout your dreams. Think I

know where you be - long. Think I know it's with me. _____ Can't you

*Let chord ring.   **Sung as written.

Outro-Chorus

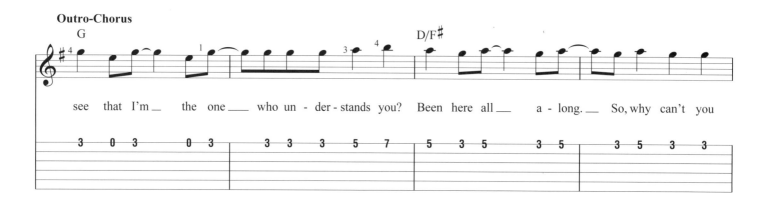

see that I'm __ the one __ who un - der - stands you? Been here all __ a - long. __ So, why can't you

see _____ you be - long __ with me? _____

***Let chord ring.

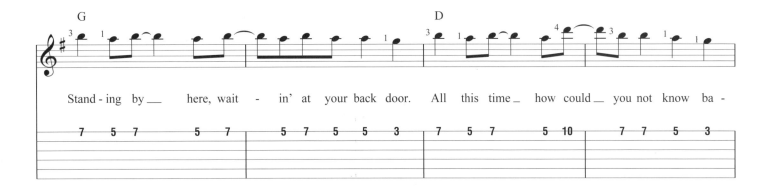

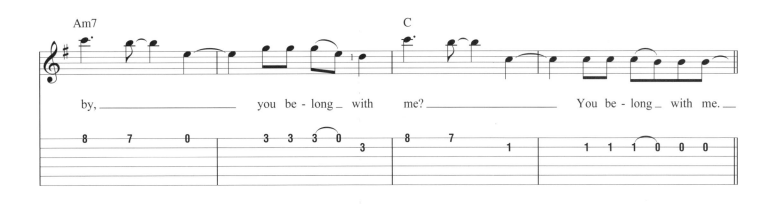

Outro

Wildest Dreams

Words and Music by Taylor Swift, Max Martin and Shellback

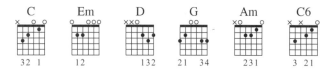

*Capo I

Strum Pattern: 4
Pick Pattern: 1

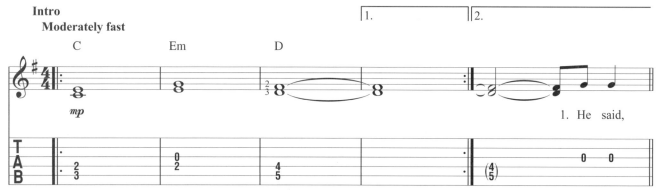

*Optional: To match recording, place capo at 1st fret.

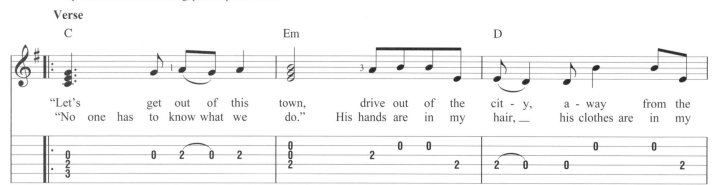

**Sung one octave higher.

hand - some as hell.   He's so bad, but he does it so well.____
hand - some as hell.   He's so bad, but he does it so well.____

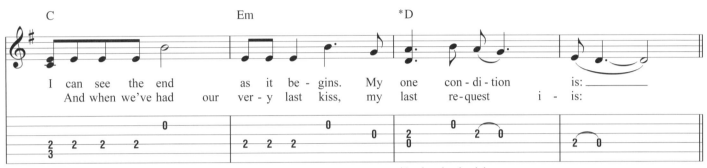

I can see the end   as it be - gins. My one con - di - tion is:____
And when we've had   our ver - y last kiss, my last re - quest i - is:

*1st time, let chord ring.
2nd time, substitute N.C.

𝄋 Chorus

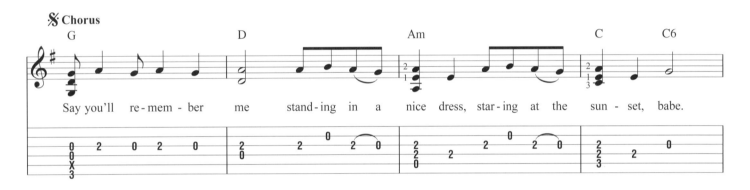

Say you'll re - mem - ber me stand - ing in a nice dress, star - ing at the sun - set, babe.

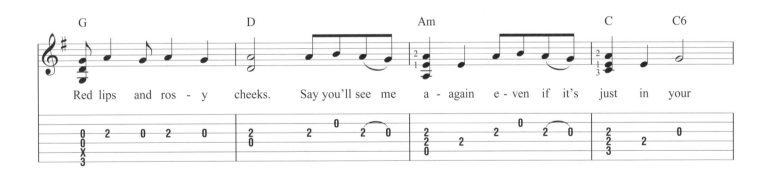

Red lips and ros - y cheeks. Say you'll see me a - again e - ven if it's just in your

3rd time, To Coda ⊕

wild - est dreams,____ ah,____ ha.____

Wild - est dreams, _____ ah, _____ ha. _____

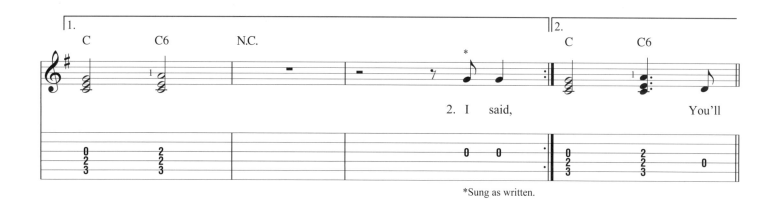

2. I said, You'll

*Sung as written.

Bridge

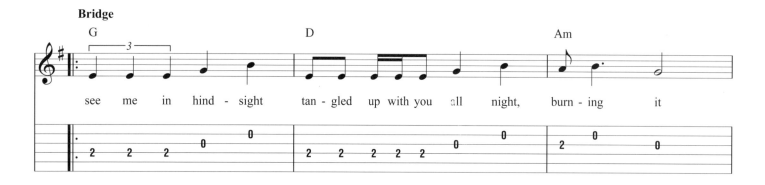

see me in hind - sight tan - gled up with you all night, burn - ing it

down. _____ Some - day when you leave me, I'll bet these mem - 'ries

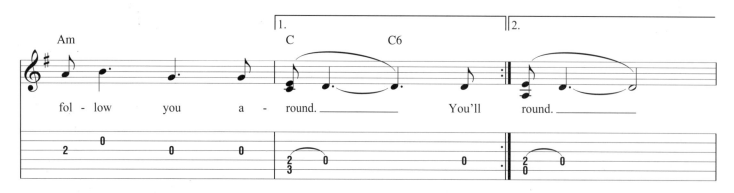

fol - low you a - round. _____ You'll round. _____

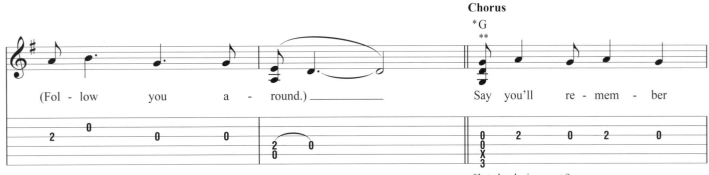

Chorus

(Fol - low you a - round.) _____ Say you'll re - mem - ber

*Let chords ring, next 9 meas.
**Sung as written, next 9 meas.

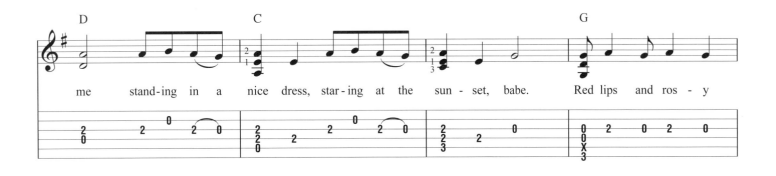

me stand-ing in a nice dress, star-ing at the sun - set, babe. Red lips and ros - y

D.S. al Coda

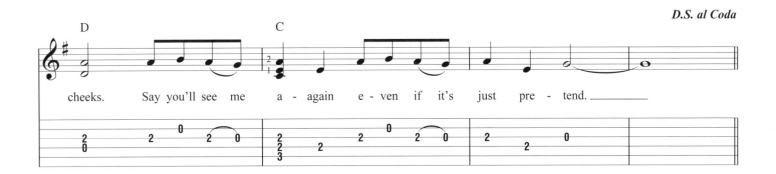

cheeks. Say you'll see me a - again e - ven if it's just pre - tend. _____

⊕ Coda

In your wild - est dreams, _____ ah, _____ ha. _____

In your wild - est dreams, _____ ah, _____ ha. _____

***Let chords ring.

115

This series features simplified arrangements with notes, tab, chord charts, and strum and pick patterns.

MIXED FOLIOS

00702287	Acoustic	$19.99
00702002	Acoustic Rock Hits for Easy Guitar	$17.99
00702166	All-Time Best Guitar Collection	$29.99
00702232	Best Acoustic Songs for Easy Guitar	$16.99
00119835	Best Children's Songs	$16.99
00703055	The Big Book of Nursery Rhymes & Children's Songs	$16.99
00698978	Big Christmas Collection	$19.99
00702394	Bluegrass Songs for Easy Guitar	$15.99
00289632	Bohemian Rhapsody	$19.99
00703387	Celtic Classics	$16.99
00224808	Chart Hits of 2016-2017	$14.99
00267383	Chart Hits of 2017-2018	$14.99
00334293	Chart Hits of 2019-2020	$16.99
00403479	Chart Hits of 2021-2022	$16.99
00702149	Children's Christian Songbook	$9.99
00702028	Christmas Classics	$9.99
00101779	Christmas Guitar	$16.99
00702141	Classic Rock	$8.95
00159642	Classical Melodies	$12.99
00253933	Disney/Pixar's Coco	$19.99
00702203	CMT's 100 Greatest Country Songs	$34.99
00702283	The Contemporary Christian Collection	$16.99
00196954	Contemporary Disney	$19.99
00702239	Country Classics for Easy Guitar	$24.99
00702257	Easy Acoustic Guitar Songs	$17.99
00702041	Favorite Hymns for Easy Guitar	$12.99
00222701	Folk Pop Songs	$19.99
00126894	Frozen	$14.99
00333922	Frozen 2	$14.99
00702286	Glee	$16.99
00702160	The Great American Country Songbook	$19.99
00702148	Great American Gospel for Guitar	$14.99
00702050	Great Classical Themes for Easy Guitar	$9.99
00148030	Halloween Guitar Songs	$17.99
00702273	Irish Songs	$14.99
00192503	Jazz Classics for Easy Guitar	$16.99
00702275	Jazz Favorites for Easy Guitar	$17.99
00702274	Jazz Standards for Easy Guitar	$19.99
00702162	Jumbo Easy Guitar Songbook	$24.99
00232285	La La Land	$16.99
00702258	Legends of Rock	$14.99
00702189	MTV's 100 Greatest Pop Songs	$34.99
00702272	1950s Rock	$16.99
00702271	1960s Rock	$16.99
00702270	1970s Rock	$24.99
00702269	1980s Rock	$16.99
00702268	1990s Rock	$24.99
00369043	Rock Songs for Kids	$14.99
00109725	Once	$14.99
00702187	Selections from O Brother Where Art Thou?	$19.99
00702178	100 Songs for Kids	$16.99
00702515	Pirates of the Caribbean	$17.99
00702125	Praise and Worship for Guitar	$14.99
00287930	Songs from A Star Is Born, The Greatest Showman, La La Land, and More Movie Musicals	$16.99
00702285	Southern Rock Hits	$12.99
00156420	Star Wars Music	$16.99
00121535	30 Easy Celtic Guitar Solos	$16.99
00244654	Top Hits of 2017	$14.99
00283786	Top Hits of 2018	$14.99
00302269	Top Hits of 2019	$14.99
00355779	Top Hits of 2020	$14.99
00374083	Top Hits of 2021	$16.99
00702294	Top Worship Hits	$17.99
00702255	VH1's 100 Greatest Hard Rock Songs	$39.99
00702175	VH1's 100 Greatest Songs of Rock and Roll	$34.99
00702253	Wicked	$12.99

ARTIST COLLECTIONS

00702267	AC/DC for Easy Guitar	$17.99
00156221	Adele – 25	$16.99
00396889	Adele – 30	$19.99
00702040	Best of the Allman Brothers	$16.99
00702865	J.S. Bach for Easy Guitar	$15.99
00702169	Best of The Beach Boys	$16.99
00702292	The Beatles — 1	$22.99
00125796	Best of Chuck Berry	$16.99
00702201	The Essential Black Sabbath	$15.99
00702250	blink-182 — Greatest Hits	$19.99
02501615	Zac Brown Band — The Foundation	$19.99
02501621	Zac Brown Band — You Get What You Give	$16.99
00702043	Best of Johnny Cash	$19.99
00702090	Eric Clapton's Best	$16.99
00702086	Eric Clapton — from the Album Unplugged	$17.99
00702202	The Essential Eric Clapton	$19.99
00702053	Best of Patsy Cline	$17.99
00222697	Very Best of Coldplay – 2nd Edition	$17.99
00702229	The Very Best of Creedence Clearwater Revival	$16.99
00702145	Best of Jim Croce	$16.99
00702278	Crosby, Stills & Nash	$12.99
14042809	Bob Dylan	$15.99
00702276	Fleetwood Mac — Easy Guitar Collection	$17.99
00139462	The Very Best of Grateful Dead	$17.99
00702136	Best of Merle Haggard	$19.99
00702227	Jimi Hendrix — Smash Hits	$19.99
00702288	Best of Hillsong United	$12.99
00702236	Best of Antonio Carlos Jobim	$15.99
00702245	Elton John — Greatest Hits 1970–2002	$19.99
00129855	Jack Johnson	$17.99
00702204	Robert Johnson	$16.99
00702234	Selections from Toby Keith — 35 Biggest Hits	$12.95
00702003	Kiss	$16.99
00702216	Lynyrd Skynyrd	$17.99
00702182	The Essential Bob Marley	$17.99
00146081	Maroon 5	$14.99
00121925	Bruno Mars – Unorthodox Jukebox	$12.99
00702248	Paul McCartney — All the Best	$14.99
00125484	The Best of MercyMe	$12.99
00702209	Steve Miller Band — Young Hearts (Greatest Hits)	$12.95
00124167	Jason Mraz	$15.99
00702096	Best of Nirvana	$17.99
00702211	The Offspring — Greatest Hits	$17.99
00138026	One Direction	$17.99
00702030	Best of Roy Orbison	$17.99
00702144	Best of Ozzy Osbourne	$14.99
00702279	Tom Petty	$17.99
00102911	Pink Floyd	$17.99
00702139	Elvis Country Favorites	$19.99
00702293	The Very Best of Prince	$22.99
00699415	Best of Queen for Guitar	$16.99
00109279	Best of R.E.M.	$14.99
00702208	Red Hot Chili Peppers — Greatest Hits	$19.99
00198960	The Rolling Stones	$17.99
00174793	The Very Best of Santana	$16.99
00702196	Best of Bob Seger	$16.99
00146046	Ed Sheeran	$19.99
00702252	Frank Sinatra — Nothing But the Best	$12.99
00702010	Best of Rod Stewart	$17.99
00702049	Best of George Strait	$17.99
00702259	Taylor Swift for Easy Guitar	$15.99
00359800	Taylor Swift – Easy Guitar Anthology	$24.99
00702260	Taylor Swift — Fearless	$14.99
00139727	Taylor Swift — 1989	$19.99
00115960	Taylor Swift — Red	$16.99
00253667	Taylor Swift — Reputation	$17.99
00702290	Taylor Swift — Speak Now	$16.99
00232849	Chris Tomlin Collection – 2nd Edition	$14.99
00702226	Chris Tomlin — See the Morning	$12.95
00148643	Train	$14.99
00702427	U2 — 18 Singles	$19.99
00702108	Best of Stevie Ray Vaughan	$17.99
00279005	The Who	$14.99
00702123	Best of Hank Williams	$15.99
00194548	Best of John Williams	$14.99
00702228	Neil Young — Greatest Hits	$17.99
00119133	Neil Young — Harvest	$16.99

Prices, contents and availability subject to change without notice.

Visit Hal Leonard online at halleonard.com

FIRST 50

Books in the First 50 series contain easy to intermediate arrangements for must-know songs. Each arrangement is simple and streamlined, yet still captures the essence of the tune.

First 50 Baroque Pieces
You Should Play on Guitar
Includes selections by Johann Sebastian Bach, Robert de Visée, Ernst Gottlieb Baron, Santiago de Murcia, Antonio Vivaldi, Sylvius Leopold Weiss, and more.
00322567 ....$14.99

First 50 Bluegrass Solos
You Should Play on Guitar
I Am a Man of Constant Sorrow • Long Journey Home • Molly and Tenbrooks • Old Joe Clark • Rocky Top • Salty Dog Blues • and more.
00298574...$16.99

First 50 Blues Songs
You Should Play on Guitar
All Your Love (I Miss Loving) • Bad to the Bone • Born Under a Bad Sign • Dust My Broom • Hoodoo Man Blues • Little Red Rooster • Love Struck Baby • Pride and Joy • Smoking Gun • Still Got the Blues • The Thrill Is Gone • You Shook Me • and more.
00235790...$17.99

First 50 Blues Turnarounds
You Should Play on Guitar
You'll learn cool turnarounds in the styles of these jazz legends: John Lee Hooker, Robert Johnson, Joe Pass, Jimmy Rogers, Hubert Sumlin, Stevie Ray Vaughan, T-Bone Walker, Muddy Waters, and more.
00277469...$14.99

First 50 Chords
You Should Play on Guitar
American Pie • Back in Black • Brown Eyed Girl • Landslide • Let It Be • Riptide • Summer of '69 • Take Me Home, Country Roads • Won't Get Fooled Again • You've Got a Friend • and more.
00300255 Guitar $12.99

First 50 Classical Pieces
You Should Play on Guitar
Includes compositions by J.S. Bach, Augustin Barrios, Matteo Carcassi, Domenico Scarlatti, Fernando Sor, Francisco Tárrega, Robert de Visée, Antonio Vivaldi and many more.
00155414 ....$16.99

First 50 Folk Songs
You Should Play on Guitar
Amazing Grace • Down by the Riverside • Home on the Range • I've Been Working on the Railroad • Kumbaya • Man of Constant Sorrow • Oh! Susanna • This Little Light of Mine • When the Saints Go Marching In • The Yellow Rose of Texas • and more.
00235868 ....$16.99

First 50 Guitar Duets
You Should Play
Chopsticks • Clocks • Eleanor Rigby • Game of Thrones Theme • Hallelujah • Linus and Lucy (from A Charlie Brown Christmas) • Memory (from Cats) • Over the Rainbow (from The Wizard of Oz) • Star Wars (Main Theme) • What a Wonderful World • You Raise Me Up • and more.
00319706...$14.99

First 50 Jazz Standards
You Should Play on Guitar
All the Things You Are • Body and Soul • Don't Get Around Much Anymore • Fly Me to the Moon (In Other Words) • The Girl from Ipanema (Garota De Ipanema) • I Got Rhythm • Laura • Misty • Night and Day • Satin Summertime • When I Fall in Love • and more.
00198594 Solo Guitar $16.99

First 50 Kids' Songs
You Should Play on Guitar
Do-Re-Mi • Hakuna Matata • Let It Go • My Favorite Things • Puff the Magic Dragon • Take Me Out to the Ball Game • Won't You Be My Neighbor? (It's a Beautiful Day in the Neighborhood) • and more.
00300500 ....$17.99

First 50 Licks
You Should Play on Guitar
Licks presented include the styles of legendary guitarists like Eric Clapton, Buddy Guy, Jimi Hendrix, B.B. King, Randy Rhoads, Carlos Santana, Stevie Ray Vaughan and many more.
00278875 Book/Online Audio..........................$14.99

First 50 Riffs
You Should Play on Guitar
All Right Now • Back in Black • Barracuda • Carry on Wayward Son • Crazy Train • La Grange • Layla • Seven Nation Army • Smoke on the Water • Sunday Bloody Sunday • Sunshine of Your Love • Sweet Home Alabama • Working Man • and more.
00277366...$17.99

First 50 Rock Songs You Should
Play on Electric Guitar
All Along the Watchtower • Beat It • Brown Eyed Girl • Cocaine • Detroit Rock City • Hallelujah • (I Can't Get No) Satisfaction • Oh, Pretty Woman • Pride and Joy • Seven Nation Army • Should I Stay or Should I Go • Smells like Teen Spirit • Smoke on the Water • When I Come Around • You Really Got Me • and more.
00131159...$16.99

First 50 Songs by the Beatles You
Should Play on Guitar
All You Need Is Love • Blackbird • Come Together • Eleanor Rigby • Hey Jude • I Want to Hold Your Hand • Let It Be • Ob-La-Di, Ob-La-Da • She Loves You • Twist and Shout • Yellow Submarine • Yesterday • and more.
00295323...$24.99

First 50 Songs
You Should Fingerpick on Guitar
Annie's Song • Blackbird • The Boxer • Classical Gas • Dust in the Wind • Fire and Rain • Greensleeves • Road Trippin' • Shape of My Heart • Tears in Heaven • Time in a Bottle • Vincent (Starry Starry Night) • and more.
00149269...$16.99

First 50 Songs You Should
Play on 12-String Guitar
California Dreamin' • Closer to the Heart • Free Fallin' • Give a Little Bit • Hotel California • Leaving on a Jet Plane • Life by the Drop • Over the Hills and Far Away • Solsbury Hill • Space Oddity • Wish You Were Here • You Wear It Well • and more.
00287559...$19.99

First 50 Songs You Should Play on
Acoustic Guitar
Against the Wind • Boulevard of Broken Dreams • Champagne Supernova • Every Rose Has Its Thorn • Fast Car • Free Fallin' • Layla • Let Her Go • Mean • One • Ring of Fire • Signs • Stairway to Heaven • Trouble • Wagon Wheel • Yellow • Yesterday • and more.
00131209 ....$16.99

First 50 Songs
You Should Play on Bass
Blister in the Sun • I Got You (I Feel Good) • Livin' on a Prayer • Low Rider • Money • Monkey Wrench • My Generation • Roxanne • Should I Stay or Should I Go • Uptown Funk • What's Going On • With or Without You • Yellow • and more.
00149189 ....$16.99

First 50 Songs
You Should Play on Solo Guitar
Africa • All of Me • Blue Skies • California Dreamin' • Change the World • Crazy • Dream a Little Dream of Me • Every Breath You Take • Hallelujah • Wonderful Tonight • Yesterday • You Raise Me Up • Your Song • and more.
00288843...$19.99

First 50 Songs
You Should Strum on Guitar
American Pie • Blowin' in the Wind • Daughter • Hey, Soul Sister • Home • I Will Wait • Losing My Religion • Mrs. Robinson • No Woman No Cry • Peaceful Easy Feeling • Rocky Mountain High • Sweet Caroline • Teardrops on My Guitar • Wonderful Tonight • and more.
00148996...$16.99

HAL•LEONARD®
www.halleonard.com

0623
014

The **Deluxe Guitar Play-Along®** series will help you play songs faster than ever before! Accurate, easy-to-read guitar tab and professional, customizable audio for 15 songs. The interactive, online audio interface includes tempo/pitch control, looping, buttons to turn instruments on or off, and guitar tab with follow-along marker.

The price of each book includes access to audio tracks online using the unique code inside. The tracks can also be downloaded and played offline. These books include *PLAYBACK+*, a multi-functional audio player that allows you to slow down audio, change pitch, set loop points, and pan left or right – available exclusively from Hal Leonard.

AUDIO ACCESS INCLUDED

1. TOP ROCK HITS
Basket Case • Black Hole Sun • Come As You Are • Do I Wanna Know? • Gold on the Ceiling • Heaven • How You Remind Me • Kryptonite • No One Knows • Plush • The Pretender • Seven Nation Army • Smooth • Under the Bridge • Yellow Ledbetter. **00244758**

2. REALLY EASY SONGS
Californication • Free Fallin' • Hey Joe • Highway to Hell • I Love Rock 'N Roll • Knockin' on Heaven's Door • La Bamba • Oh, Pretty Woman • Should I Stay or Should I Go • Smells Like Teen Spirit. • and more. **00244877**

3. ACOUSTIC SONGS
All Apologies • Banana Pancakes • Crash Into Me • Good Riddance (Time of Your Life) • Hallelujah • Hey There Delilah • Ho Hey • I Will Wait • I'm Yours • Iris • More Than Words • No Such Thing • Photograph • What I Got • Wonderwall. **00244709**

4. THE BEATLES
All My Loving • And I Love Her • Back in the U.S.S.R. • Don't Let Me Down • Get Back • A Hard Day's Night • Here Comes the Sun • I Will • In My Life • Let It Be • Michelle • Paperback Writer • Revolution • While My Guitar Gently Weeps • Yesterday. **00244968**

5. BLUES STANDARDS
Crosscut Saw • Double Trouble • Every Day I Have the Blues • Going Down • I'm Tore Down • I'm Your Hoochie Coochie Man • Killing Floor • Let Me Love You Baby • Pride and Joy • Sweet Home Chicago • and more. **00245090**

6. RED HOT CHILI PEPPERS
The Adventures of Rain Dance Maggie • Breaking the Girl • Can't Stop • Dani California • Dark Necessities • Give It Away • My Friends • Otherside • Road Trippin' • Scar Tissue • Snow (Hey Oh) • Suck My Kiss • Tell Me Baby • Under the Bridge • The Zephyr Song. **00245089**

7. CLASSIC ROCK
Baba O'Riley • Born to Be Wild • Comfortably Numb • Dream On • Fortunate Son • Heartbreaker • Hotel California • Jet Airliner • More Than a Feeling • Old Time Rock & Roll • Rhiannon • Runnin' Down a Dream • Start Me Up • Sultans of Swing • Sweet Home Alabama. **00248381**

8. OZZY OSBOURNE
Bark at the Moon • Close My Eyes Forever • Crazy Train • Dreamer • Mama, I'm Coming Home • No More Tears • Over the Mountain • Perry Mason • Rock 'N Roll Rebel • Shot in the Dark • and more. **00248413**

9. ED SHEERAN
The A Team • All of the Stars • Castle on the Hill • Don't • Drunk • Galway Girl • Give Me Love • How Would You Feel (Paean) • I See Fire • Lego House • Make It Rain • Perfect • Photograph • Shape of You • Thinking Out Loud. **00248439**

10. CHRISTMAS SONGS
Blue Christmas • Christmas Time Is Here • Do You Hear What I Hear • Feliz Navidad • Have Yourself a Merry Little Christmas • I'll Be Home for Christmas • Little Saint Nick • Please Come Home for Christmas • Santa Baby • White Christmas • Winter Wonderland • and more. **00278088**

11. PINK FLOYD
Another Brick in the Wall, Part 2 • Brain Damage • Breathe • Comfortably Numb • Goodbye Blue Sky • Have a Cigar • Hey You • Learning to Fly • Money • Mother • Run like Hell • Time • Welcome to the Machine • Wish You Were Here • Young Lust. **00278487**

12. THREE-CHORD SONGS
Ain't No Sunshine • Bad Moon Rising • Beverly Hills • Evil Ways • Just the Way You Are • Ring of Fire • Twist and Shout • What I Got • What's Up • and more. **00278488**

13. FOUR-CHORD SONGS
Chasing Cars • Cruise • Demons • Hand in My Pocket • Hey, Soul Sister • Hey Ya! • If I Had $1,000,000 • Riptide • Rude • Save Tonight • Steal My Girl • Steal My Kisses • 3 AM • Toes • Zombie. **00287263**

14. BOB SEGER
Against the Wind • Feel like a Number • The Fire down Below • Fire Lake • Her Strut • Hollywood Nights • Like a Rock • Mainstreet • Night Moves • Old Time Rock & Roll • Rock and Roll Never Forgets • Still the Same • Sunspot Baby • Turn the Page • You'll Accomp'ny Me. **00287279**

15. METAL ANTHOLOGY
Ace of Spades • The Devil in I • Down with the Sickness • Hallowed Be Thy Name • Master of Puppets • No More Tears • Painkiller • Rainbow in the Dark • Sober • Walk • War Pigs (Interpolating Luke's Wall) • and more. **00287269**

18. KISS
Christine Sixteen • Cold Gin • Detroit Rock City • Deuce • Firehouse • God of Thunder • Heaven's on Fire • I Stole Your Love • I Was Made for Lovin' You • Lick It Up • Love Gun • Rock and Roll All Nite • Shock Me • Shout It Out Loud • Strutter. **00288989**

19. CHRISTMAS CLASSICS
Away in a Manger • Deck the Hall • The First Noel • Go, Tell It on the Mountain • Hark! the Herald Angels Sing • It Came upon the Midnight Clear • Jingle Bells • O Holy Night • O Little Town of Bethlehem • Silent Night • and more. **00294776**

21. NEIL YOUNG
Cowgirl in the Sand • Down by the River • Harvest Moon • Heart of Gold • Like a Hurricane • Old Man • Only Love Can Break Your Heart • Rockin' in the Free World • Southern Man • and more. **00322911**

24. JIMI HENDRIX
Angel • Crosstown Traffic • Fire • Foxey Lady • Freedom • Hear My Train a Comin' • Izabella • Little Wing • Manic Depression • Purple Haze • Red House • Star Spangled Banner (Instrumental) • Stone Free • Voodoo Child (Slight Return) • The Wind Cries Mary. **00324610**

HAL•LEONARD®

Visit halleonard.com for more information

Prices, contents, and availability subject to change without notice.

0222
467